Published by Jossey-Bass
A Wiley Imprint
989 Market Street, San Francisco, CA 94103-1741—www.josseybass.com

Jossey-Bass books and products are available through most bookstores. To contact Jossey-Bass directly call our Customer Care Department within the U.S. at 800-956-7739, outside the U.S. at 317-572-3986, or fax 317-572-4002.

Jossey-Bass also publishes its books in a variety of electronic formats. Some content that appears in print may not be available in electronic books.

Library of Congress Cataloging-in-Publication Data
Roberts, Dennis C., Ph. D.
  Deeper learning in leadership : helping college students find the potential within / Dennis C. Roberts.—1st ed.
    p. cm.—(The Jossey-Bass higher and adult education series)
  Includes bibliographical references and index.
  ISBN 978-0-7879-8585-1 (cloth)
    1. Education, Higher—Social aspects—United States. 2. Leadership—Study and teaching (Higher)—United States. 3. Social values—Study and teaching (Higher)—United States. I. Title.
  LC191.94.R63 2007
  378.19'8—dc22
                                                                    2007021304

Printed in the United States of America
FIRST EDITION
HB *Printing*   10 9 8 7 6 5 4 3 2 1

JB JOSSEY-BASS

Deeper Learning in Leadership

Helping College Students Find the Potential Within

Dennis C. Roberts

BICENTENNIAL
1807
WILEY
2007
BICENTENNIAL

Published by Jossey-Bass
A Wiley Imprint
989 Market Street, San Francisco, CA 94103-1741—www.josseybass.com

Jossey-Bass books and products are available through most bookstores. To contact Jossey-Bass directly call our Customer Care Department within the U.S. at 800-956-7739, outside the U.S. at 317-572-3986, or fax 317-572-4002.

Jossey-Bass also publishes its books in a variety of electronic formats. Some content that appears in print may not be available in electronic books.

Library of Congress Cataloging-in-Publication Data
Roberts, Dennis C., Ph. D.
  Deeper learning in leadership : helping college students find the potential within / Dennis C. Roberts.—1st ed.
    p. cm.—(The Jossey-Bass higher and adult education series)
  Includes bibliographical references and index.
  ISBN 978-0-7879-8585-1 (cloth)
  1. Education, Higher—Social aspects—United States. 2. Leadership—Study and teaching (Higher)—United States. 3. Social values—Study and teaching (Higher)—United States. I. Title.
  LC191.94.R63 2007
  378.19'8—dc22
                                                                2007021304

Printed in the United States of America
FIRST EDITION
HB *Printing*   10 9 8 7 6 5 4 3 2 1

Contents

Esther McDonald Lloyd-Jones (1901–1991)—Dedicated to the memory and vision of a pioneer in student personnel work. She was an artist, scholar, advocate, mentor, wife, and mother. She tirelessly sought to push the boundaries of knowledge in student affairs practice until her last days.

Foreword

Dennis Roberts's new book is such a welcome addition to the burgeoning literature on leadership. His definition of leadership as *conviction in action*, simple and elegant, manages to embody several basic principles of effective leadership. *Conviction*, for example, not only requires a certain level of self-awareness of our personal values, but also touches base with the passions that ultimately lead us to *action* on behalf of others, a better society, and a better world. *Conviction*, in other words, speaks to connecting with who we are, what we value and care about, and how we exercise leadership toward goals that serve others, as well as our institutions.

One of the unique features of Roberts's approach is his attempt to synthesize diverse views of theorists in a variety of fields. Thus, in advocating what he calls "deeper learning in leadership" and an emphasis on "wholeness," Roberts argues that one needs to consider three paths: presence, flow, and oscillation. In exploring the implications of presence he proposes a novel approach that integrates four diverse theoretical perspectives: the six-stage progression of Senge, Scharmer, Jaworski, and Flowers; Perry's nine developmental stages; Wilber's evolutionary model; and the "7 C's" of the Social Change Model of Leadership Development. The second path, flow, derives from the work of Csikszentmihalyi; oscillation is based on the writings of Palmer and Schwartz and Loehr.

Whenever we think about, observe, teach, or practice leadership, the critical question for us is, Leadership to what end? Seeking answers to such a question inevitably forces us to deal with issues of values, ethics, and the use or misuse of power. What are the values that guide leadership? Are leadership actions directed toward ends that are ethical? Does the leader use or misuse the power vested in her?

According to Roberts, ethical or deeper leadership also helps us make meaning of our work and strengthens our sense of interconnectedness. But in addressing questions of ends or goals, we also have to deal with the leadership *process*, because our means necessarily become part of our ends. And focusing on the ends or goals of leadership necessarily raises a number of fundamental questions: How do we go inward to examine the values that we hold most dear? How do we achieve greater wholeness and integration in our personal and professional lives? How do we become more caring toward each other and our environment? How, in short, do we touch base with our spirituality, the domain of our life that pertains to ultimate meaning and purpose?

As paradigms have shifted from hierarchical to more collaborative or "servant" models of leadership, we have also witnessed the emergence of new studies and books connecting leadership with spirituality. It seems to us that this trend has been fueled by the recognition that we need to foster a greater sense of community in organizations, to promote the notion of leadership as service, and to see leadership as a form of meaning making.

In a recent interview (*Shambhala Sun*, Jan. 2001), Peter Senge and Margaret Wheatley, two of our most thoughtful contemporary scholars of organizations and of change in organizations, reflected on the interconnections between leadership and spirituality. Senge sees "leadership as being deeply personal and inherently collective." This personal dimension of leadership, according to Wheatley, calls for being aware, listening attentively, and then letting go. Both of these scholars believe that facilitating change in organizations requires the leader to understand her own habitual patterns and, if necessary, to be willing to move into a different way of being. To do so demands reflection, a careful look into who we are and our habitual patterns of behavior, and, in turn, a willingness to make a shift in thought and behavior, a shift both in our beliefs and in our actions.

To begin to connect leadership with spirituality and thus understand how spirituality and its cultivation can enable us to practice leadership that represents *conviction*, it is important to attend to our values and ideals and to cultivate a clear sense of meaning and purpose in our lives. Although many have argued that leadership is *doing*, and spirituality is *being*, it is in connecting what we do with what we are that helps us see how leadership interfaces with spirituality.

More than a decade ago, we had the pleasure of working with Dennis Roberts and several other wonderful colleagues on a two-year project that led to the development of the Social Change Model of Leadership Development. This model, as elaborated here by Roberts, promotes such spiritual qualities as respect, human goodness, connection, integrity, equity, humility, service, and personal growth. Thus, to be able to shape a *common purpose* (one of the 7 C's in the Social Change model) requires that group members respect each other and believe in the basic goodness of others. For the group to work *collaboratively*, members need to work on personal growth (*consciousness of self*), to have integrity, to be authentic (*congruent*), and to feel connected—all essential qualities needed to sustain the collective group effort. And, of course, it is humility that enables group members to express differing points of view (*controversy with civility*). These leadership qualities can be cultivated by doing the inner work, by recognizing and nurturing one's spirituality.

We salute our friend and colleague Dennis Roberts for helping to move the leadership conversation to a new level and for providing the educational community with some theoretical perspectives and practical tools for fostering leadership development as *conviction in action*.

Helen S. Astin and Alexander W. Astin
Los Angeles

Preface

This book began in my head over a decade ago. The first seeds were planted by colleagues who urged me to update and publish a second edition of *Student Leadership Programs in Higher Education* (Roberts, 1981). I resisted the notion for years, knowing that the things I continued to learn about leadership made it impossible to stop long enough to provide a new summary piece about how leadership could be fostered.

A second theme in my professional life has been the study of student personnel work in the twentieth century. I first became interested in the origins of student affairs when I became acquainted with Dr. Esther Lloyd-Jones in 1986. I had read of Esther's legacy and had the chance to meet her while making arrangements for the past-presidents' breakfast for the 1987 American College Personnel Association convention. That year marked the fiftieth anniversary of the publication of the *Student Personnel Point of View*, of which Esther was one of the primary authors. Finding her beyond fascinating, I began studying Esther by reviewing her publications, interviewing her, and corresponding with her. This growing relationship resulted in a fundamentally new understanding of student affairs work and a desire to bring attention to one of Esther's most interesting publications, *Student Personnel Work as Deeper Teaching* (Lloyd-Jones & Smith, 1954).

Deeper Learning in Leadership explores the two themes of fostering leadership learning and advocating for student affairs practice in ways consistent with the founding philosophers' views.

In addition to these themes, *Deeper Learning in Leadership* is focused on helping students. Students struggle to understand how to make the most of the collegiate experience. They search for meaning and they strive to learn how to be effective contributors and leaders. They see flawed leadership in many places around them, and they wonder if that's the way it has to be. They examine their own experience for clues about what they need to learn in order to be different from, and better than, those who preceded them. Students look for good company on the often difficult path of leadership. Current students and our graduates tell us of the search to find commitments that will allow them to make their greatest contributions to the world. They also express their desire to be more effective in striving to fulfill their life's purpose.

Many books are written about theory and its development, and others focus on practice. However, some of the most fulfilling experiences in education occur as we work to bridge the two. This book attempts to begin closing the gap between theory and practice. Every time I started to tackle writing *Deeper Learning in Leadership*, the fear of not including all the latest theory and examples stopped me in my tracks. The fact was that the pace never slowed, and today I know a great deal more than I did a decade ago, but I also have even more unanswered questions that will linger indefinitely.

I have chosen to write in narrative form, using my observations and experiences liberally throughout the chapters that follow. This is not to imply that everyone's experience is the same—clearly it is not. By being transparent about my own experience, struggles, and insight, I hope to demonstrate that leadership learning is not only a journey for our students but, indeed, a constant journey for those of us who study, teach, and develop leadership with students. I write from the perspective of a student affairs administrator as well as a faculty member who has taught both undergraduate and graduate students throughout my career. It is this dual role that calls me to advocate that leadership learning be addressed as a mutual goal among faculty, staff, and students.

Leadership captivated me over thirty years ago. I remain fascinated by the work of others and by students' wonderful journeys of understanding leadership. However, I am concerned—concerned that our work is not reaching deeply enough into the minds and hearts of our students. It is this concern that drew me to write *Deeper Learning in Leadership*.

In the chapters that follow, I will propose models of learning and leadership to use in deepening our work. I will provide summaries, not exhaustive but introductory, of widely used leadership theories, and I will propose other models with which you are likely unfamiliar. After providing a landscape view, I will propose a perspective of leadership and a process of discovering it that educators can use to deepen students' experiences. This model, deeper leadership, is a stimulus for reflection. If you find it helpful as you frame the work you pursue with students, so much the better. However, the purpose is more to encourage you to find a framework that makes sense to you, the institution you serve, and the students who are the beneficiaries of leadership learning. At its core, the deeper leadership perspective is one that, if utilized as a consistent backdrop for your thinking, can create self-monitoring and self-correcting systems that encourage ethical practices in leadership. The work of discovering the potential within each individual requires all members of a campus community—students, faculty, and staff alike—to engage in the critical examination of leadership on a daily basis. Through broad-based and widespread examination, we all gain the opportunity and responsibility to question the conduct of others, engage in substantive conversations, and reflect on the impact and ethical implications of our actions. Such an environment would have a chance of fostering the broader and deeper leadership capacity that we need in our institutions, communities, nation, and around the globe.

Chapter Sequence and Summaries

Deeper Learning in Leadership is written with a purposeful progression of chapters, but you need not read each chapter successively. Chapter Five, "Accessing Purpose and Voice for Deeper Leadership," is the culmination of *Deeper Learning in Leadership's* argument, and all the other chapters either build to or are derived from it.

The Potential of Deeper Learning

Chapter One charts the historical evolution of higher education in North America, including how it is organized and staffed. This historical summary eventually turns to the emergence of student personnel work in the early twentieth century, how this grew out of institutional need, and how this influenced the organization of contemporary colleges and universities. The philosophies and models that emerged made sense in their time. By contrast to prevailing trends in the middle and late twentieth century, Esther Lloyd-Jones, to whom this book is dedicated, posed a model of engaged learning and mutual work among faculty and staff. She had a vision of higher education that met students' needs while exploiting the opportunities for learning throughout our institutions. The chapter concludes by citing research and models that substantiate the need for faculty and staff to work together to enhance both learning and leadership.

The Context of Leadership Learning

Chapter Two summarizes the emergence of leadership development as a field. One of the challenges facing an evolving field is that there are disparate views of what leadership is and how it might be taught or cultivated. This chapter prepares you for conversations about what leadership is and why it should have a place as an area of focus in the academy, and concludes with an appeal for faculty and staff to join together in studying and developing leadership. This chapter also proposes that leadership learning could become an initiative that would create new models for collegiate communities, models where students' learning inside and outside of class would be in constant dialogue.

Leadership Theory in Use

Not all faculty and staff can stay abreast of the current leadership research and theories. This problem is exacerbated by the fact that the popularity of leadership has contributed to a profusion of "airplane reading" that may or may not have a basis in research or grounding in an intentional philosophy.

Chapter Three summarizes the evolution of leadership thought in the twentieth century. Several current and most frequently used theories in campus programs and courses are summarized and implications of their use outlined. Understanding the research and theory of leadership informs the deeper conversation about which models to use and allows those planning courses and experiences to identify those theories that are likely to be most credible and useful. The theory summaries in Chapter Three are useful as an aid in analyzing the assumptions and values we have about leadership, allowing us to select those theories that align with them.

Preparing Leadership for the Future

Choosing leadership theories that fit your campus context and your program needs is a challenge when the world is changing so rapidly. One way of selecting a model is to consider approaches that address the mismatch between students' learning and the challenges of the workplace and communities of the future.

Chapter Four introduces the Making the Match research and the concerns employers have with the skills and capacities of college graduates. Leadership and organization theories that can be used to close this gap are explained. I propose several strategies for helping students move through a progressive leadership identity and, ultimately, for closing the gap and helping students determine how they can contribute positively to a changing world.

Accessing Purpose and Voice for Deeper Leadership

Learning to be more observant, suspend judgment, find purpose, and maintain it over time is a challenge for young adult students and mature educators and professionals alike. The primary obstacles are habits of busy-ness that perpetuate quick and mindless behavior.

Chapter Five proposes a way of looking at leadership that is not dissimilar from many other definitions except that it is simpler. This interpretation portrays leadership that ultimately is focused on the common good, although it recognizes that bad leadership is a reality all around us. A cyclical and life model of learning about leadership is proposed that combines the ideas of presence, flow, and oscillation. I describe these three broad areas in detail and provide examples of how they might be manifest in students' and our experiences, if students could be encouraged to slow down, learn about themselves, and acquire insights to enhance their self-knowledge and effectiveness.

Leadership Program Design and Continuous Improvement

Presence, flow, and oscillation are concepts that could help educators formulate a comprehensive curricular and cocurricular model of leadership. However, most campuses will want to create their own models. Engaging campus constituencies in this work is not easy.

Chapter Six refers to a number of resources useful for formulating ideas about a comprehensive campus leadership initiative. Insightful planners will recognize the uniqueness of their campus environment and the faculty, staff, and students who inhabit it and thus will seek to implement theories and models that reflect the specific values of the campus and the nature of the students. This chapter describes the dynamics of planning or refreshing a comprehensive leadership program.

Innovations to Deepen Leadership

Where do you look for ideas that are tried and true or that are the latest and greatest, ready for experimentation? The first place we usually look is to our colleagues on campus or elsewhere. New and mature programs alike need stimuli and ideas to keep them new, fresh, and relevant.

Chapter Seven provides a variety of ideas that can be used in the design of comprehensive leadership learning or in the renewal or redesign of an existing program. These are positioned within the presence, flow, and oscillation models, but many of the ideas can be adapted within other comprehensive models as well.

Challenges and Opportunities in Deepening Leadership

Chapter Eight seeks to integrate the previous chapters while maintaining a commitment to realism. Leadership learning is not easy for students. It is not easy for faculty and staff either. The environments in which we work have more than a little dysfunction to them. Learning to understand our campus settings, acquiring a thirst for knowledge, and remaining flexible and open to change are lessons that students, faculty, and staff could all benefit from learning. This chapter reflects an honest perspective that I hope you will read again and again when you are celebrating or when you are licking your wounds. Both are worthy of your time.

On with the Story

Deeper Learning in Leadership is a resource to formulate ways to deepen the influence of leadership learning in our institutions. Given the expansion of leadership programs throughout higher education in the last thirty years and the hope that these will continue to thrive, I propose that it is time to dig deeper for new ways to enhance our impact. This book was written to promote new perspectives and possibilities about leadership. Deeper learning and deeper leadership are essential to the future welfare of higher education and the businesses, organizations, and communities in which college graduates will serve.

This is a story of creation. It is based on the belief that our models of learning and leadership are intertwined and that to be successful in both, we have to consider new ways of working together.

New and mutual work can renew our learning communities, and this work can create the lifelong learning commitment ultimately sought by any of us who have dedicated even a portion of our personal or professional lives to the study of leadership.

Deeper Learning in Leadership is intended as a stimulus to encourage you to think carefully about the awesome responsibility we face in developing young people's leadership capacity so that they may meet and engage in a complex and challenging world. Read on with curious and critical lenses and embrace the question, "Are we doing enough to foster the deeper leadership that our communities and globe so desperately need?"

Acknowledgments

I had the extraordinary opportunity to begin my journey in understanding leadership and leadership learning when I was invited by Drury Bagwell to join him in the activities office at the University of Maryland in 1976. Dru had a vision of establishing a leadership program and asked William L. "Bud" Thomas Jr., who was vice chancellor of student affairs, to support this initiative. Not having any formal and deep understanding of leadership at the time, I sought to find colleagues who were more informed about it. I turned to the American College Personnel Association's (ACPA) Commission IV. Had Dru and Bud not had faith in me and had ACPA not provided a place for a young student affairs professional to get involved and to explore new and different ideas about practice, my professional life would have been totally different. I thank these two individuals and ACPA for providing the foundation for a lifelong love affair with my work.

While exploring how leadership learning might be enhanced, I also had the great opportunity to work toward my doctorate under the supervision of student development theory's most eloquent and thoughtful advocate: L. Lee Knefelkamp. Studying with Lee and joining together with fellow doctoral students Ron Slepitza and Linda Clement provided the support and the challenge to know my work deeply and to have the conviction never to let go of what I learned in graduate school.

Susan Komives has been a trusted and always generous colleague. Getting acquainted with Susan through ACPA governance work and later in our mutual exploration of leadership resulted in a deep and lasting respect, the likes of which legions of University of Maryland graduates now enjoy.

Alexander "Sandy" Astin and Helen "Lena" Astin convened an amazing group of professionals in the mid-1990s to explore how leadership development outside of class might be enhanced. This group created the Social Change Model of Leadership Development, a model that cleared the way for leadership development to be available for all students, regardless of their previous experience in leadership or learning. Sandy and Lena's gracious guidance and sponsorship changed every one of us who served on the "Ensemble" who discerned the Social Change model from our own experience and discovery of self.

Myrtis Powell invited me to leave the life of a small-college dean to join a remarkable institution in 1994. Miami University was celebrated as an Involving College and a public Ivy, and it has provided leadership learning opportunity for its students for decades. Yet, Myrtis's vision was to expand beyond the privileged few, thus allowing for the creation of one of the first comprehensive and inclusive leadership programs in the United States. Upon Myrtis's departure, Richard Nault's continuing sponsorship provided so many opportunities for me at Miami. He supported my undergraduate and graduate teaching, and he pushed me to explore the ways in which our leadership emphasis could break the conventional boundaries of academic and student affairs.

Sue Treadway has been my administrative assistant for most of the time I've been at Miami University. She is deeply committed to her work and serving others. I could not survive a day without her support.

Then there are the students and other colleagues who push me to learn more and explore more deeply what we seek to accomplish in leadership. For over thirty years I've been involved with hundreds, perhaps thousands, of students who joined me as partners in learning. My unwillingness to give them easy answers did not unnerve them—it empowered them. Their voices and concerns are peppered throughout the examples noted in this book. The more recent work I've done with graduate student and other colleagues has been amazing. Two particular colleagues were instrumental in helping make *Deeper Learning in Leadership* a reality. David Stanfield helped me complete early research for the book and encouraged me to move forward with the proposal. Kari Taylor provided incredible journalistic editing support as I moved through work on this manuscript. Kari's gift as a gentle and discerning journalist transformed my writing. Had she not given untold hours to reviewing drafts, *Deeper Learning in Leadership* would never have made it to press.

Finally, my family has tolerated my fascination with my work and leadership, and they have inspired me along the way. My mother, Maxine Peters, who is nearing her ninetieth year, has survived life experiences that would have made many cynical, yet she remains positive and eager to serve others. My wife, Diane, and daughters, Devin and Darbi, are the inspiration of my life. They all serve as teaching examples. My daughters have been my human development and leadership experiments as long as they can remember. Diane pursues her work with special needs sixth graders in ways that convince me that conviction and purpose are the only way we can sustain a life worth living.

All these people—family, colleagues, and friends—have been good company for the journey of life. To think that I could repay any of them for their support is a hopeless dream. Knowing that, I offer only my unending thanks.

The Author

Dr. Denny Roberts is associate vice president for student affairs at Miami University in Oxford, Ohio. He is an adjunct faculty member in the Department of Educational Leadership. In 1985–86 he was president of the American College Personnel Association (ACPA) and is now a Senior Scholar. ACPA bestowed its 2006 Esther Lloyd-Jones Professional Service Award on Roberts for sustained and visionary contributions to the field of student affairs. Roberts is a lead facilitator and member of the board of trustees for LeaderShape, Inc., which provides the LeaderShape Institute at its national site in Champaign, Illinois, and at over sixty other campuses throughout the nation. He is also a member of the International Leadership Association and the National Association of Student Personnel Administrators. Roberts is a regular presenter at conferences, and writes and speaks about leadership, community, and the origins of student personnel work in the twentieth century.

The Jossey-Bass
Higher and Adult Education Series

1

Introduction and Potential
of Deeper Learning

Learning and the assumed enhancement of leadership capability have been linked as one of the primary purposes of higher education all the way back to the origins of colonial colleges in the United States. These origins can be traced even further back to European traditions of education. For most of higher education's history, however, the link between learning and leadership has been implicit rather than explicit.

Our experiences and more recent research that documents and critiques the outcomes of higher education now demonstrate that the leadership learning that was assumed to be taking place may not have been happening to the degree we hoped. In addition, the complexity of higher education today and the breadth of the student populations we serve call us to consider more carefully, and take more seriously, the mission of fostering leadership potential in all students.

In the chapters that follow, I will address how our views of learning and leadership have changed, and show how these ideas need to continue to change. Most important, I hope that our commitments as students, scholars, and leadership advocates will bring us to a shared perspective that higher education is a vital and fertile holding environment for leadership learning among young adults.

This chapter and Chapters Two through Eight will explore the evolution of higher education and how its growing complexity resulted in organizational and mental models that may now compromise our effectiveness in the future. Although it may seem odd to begin with the history of our institutions' purposes and approaches,

I make the case that if we continue to accept our campuses as they are, we may miss essential insights that will allow us to leap forward in the twenty-first century. The expansion of higher education in the late nineteenth century and its explosion in the mid-twentieth century resulted in models that worked in their day. However, maintaining these same models without reexamining them in the context of today's changing needs may prove disastrous. As the content of learning has expanded to unforeseen proportions, and our search for knowledge becomes ever more complex, it is evident that we need to establish new approaches to learning. We need to find ways to foster a level of learning that pushes us so deeply into our own questions that the conclusions are unforgettable.

Striving for deeper learning may have inadvertently stimulated much of our quest to understand leadership, a quest I describe in Chapter Two. As colleges and universities began to pay greater and more explicit attention to leadership in the later twentieth century, leadership learning evolved into one of the hottest topics on our campuses. These early days of more intentional and comprehensive understanding in leadership learning emerged within the organizational and learning assumptions of the industrial and post–World War II eras. As more leadership scholars became involved and new theories emerged, campus leadership programs and models have attempted to incorporate the latest theoretical understandings. However, some of these programs have become strangely disconnected and sometimes inconsistent with the emerging theories. The leadership theories in widest use, summarized in Chapter Three, and the newer models described in Chapter Four have established a foundation that will allow us to move to what I believe is of ultimate importance—what I refer to as deeper leadership.

There is considerable debate about what defines leaders and leadership. Although this debate is important for scholars and will ultimately help us arrive at a fuller and more effective means of understanding leadership, it sometimes results in obscuring the practical and transcendent truths of our own experience in leadership.

This book proposes a definition that is as simple as any I've seen. It is so simple that you may initially find that you are skeptical about its relevance. However, I will build a case that this definition will bring us to an understanding of leadership that will explore some of the most important issues we face in leadership learning. The definition I propose and will explain in much greater detail in Chapter Five is that leadership is no more nor less than *conviction in action.*

Leadership as conviction in action requires that we take a careful look at ourselves. This introspection draws those interested in leadership into finding a way to access purpose and voice for this deeper leadership. Conviction comes from small steps that take us out of our routine ways of seeing the world, exposing us to new possibilities and bringing us to a depth of perspective that is more authentic, believable, and trustworthy. Chapter Five explains the personal journey involved in discovering conviction, following its call to action, and working with and through others to bring about positive change.

To bring us full circle in leadership learning, Chapters Six and Seven describe tools that can help deepen this learning. I also provide examples that have been found to help students develop greater leadership insight and capacity. Chapter Eight concludes an exploration of deeper learning and deeper leadership that will help you respond to the following four questions, which are proposed as a framework to guide our continuing journey in this book as well as your journey in fostering deeper leadership learning among students. First, what is leadership? Second, where is our leadership most needed? Third, how do we discover, pursue, and renew purpose in our own and others' lives? Finally, how do we help students embrace the importance of understanding leadership and searching for its origins in themselves?

The Purposes of Higher Education

Graduation from an institution of higher education is one of the hallmarks of success across many cultures around the globe.

Students and families alike believe that being granted a degree from a college or university is a ticket to success and a more fulfilling life. Many perceive that higher education is a natural and necessary next step beyond secondary education and that three of its primary purposes should be to foster an appreciation of the knowledge of the ages, to create a thirst for deeper understanding, and to cultivate character in graduates (Thelin, 2003). Ideally, after students complete their degrees, they will go into the world to serve others, to be successful in business and the professions, and to live fuller and more complete lives.

Although many idealize higher learning as a place that cultivates intellect, forges character, and leads to gainful employment for all citizens, others criticize institutions of higher learning as ivory towers that privilege the elite and isolate students from the real world. Even when learning is perceived to be disconnected from the realities of daily life, most of us cannot bear to abandon the belief that higher education should transform both individuals and communities. For many, even though higher education provides a path toward fulfillment of the American dream, this path may also lead young adults away from the roots that formed the dream.

Americans both revere and challenge the purposes of our institutions. Ehrlich (1997, p. 232) notes the compelling questions of "What should be learned? What should be the learning process?" The answers to these questions could help resolve the confusion and dissent among consumers and public policymakers alike. There are many other reasons for the confusion over the purposes of higher education. Perhaps the diversity of types of colleges and universities makes it difficult to perceive an overriding purpose; liberal arts colleges, land-grant universities, research universities, community colleges, technological institutes, and others are all different forms of what we generally see as constituting the higher education community. Perhaps the outcomes of higher education are simply not quantifiable in ways that allow proponents to document its impact. More germane to this chapter, perhaps higher education has emerged with organizational, governance, and human complexities that are unexplainable or do not make sense.

This chapter provides brief insights into the historical context of higher education in the United States, especially its expanding appeal to more diverse and greater numbers of students. We will look at the challenges faced by larger and more complex institutions to provide high-quality and deeper educational experiences, and explore how the student personnel movement in the early twentieth century responded to this challenge. Finally, I propose that the goal of fostering leadership in students cannot be fulfilled without attention to the variables that deepen learning throughout the academy.

Expanding the Role and Reach of Higher Education

The collegiate style of learning in the United States during the eighteenth and nineteenth centuries was substantially derived from the English models of Oxford and Cambridge (Rudolph, 1962). Colleges were established in protected pastoral settings where intellectual and social learning could be incorporated and where faculty were deeply involved in the lives of their students. This style of education was available primarily to an elite class of men who could afford or who needed this type of education to advance in the gentrified or professional circles in which they operated.

In the late nineteenth century, other types of educational institutions burst on the scene that broadened higher learning opportunities for women, for men not from privileged backgrounds, and for more culturally diverse groups (Thelin, 2003). The conclusion of the Civil War and the economic challenges associated with recovery stimulated the creation of additional colleges and universities, and a sense of social responsibility supported the establishment of institutions to serve women and cultural groups. As the types of colleges and universities expanded, so did enrollments and the complexity of the institutions required to serve these greater numbers. Students became very active in creating experiences that took place outside of class and outside the confines and supervision of colleges—including sports, literary societies, newspapers, fraternities, sororities, and others. Once these activities became more influential in students' lives, they fell under closer institutional scrutiny, and, in some cases, there were attempts to banish or control them.

One very significant exception to the trend of monitoring and supporting activities outside of class was the research university model. Based on the great German universities of the nineteenth century, such well-known and elite institutions as Johns Hopkins, Clark, and Chicago focused primarily on the creation and acquisition of knowledge; undergraduate life and personal matters were viewed as inconsequential to the much more important goal of cultivating the intellect. This philosophy stood in stark contrast to the more holistic focus of liberal arts colleges and populist universities, which subscribed to a pedagogy that was constructed around lecture as the primary interaction between students and faculty and was based on acquisition of factual knowledge and the assumption that objective truth was learning's ultimate purpose. However, the Germanic model and its focus on scientific method and discovery of knowledge had a profound impact on all colleges and universities.

The combination of reactions to the Germanic model and the establishment of other, more complex institutions set the stage for a new phenomenon. Deans were placed in a number of prominent institutions (Dean LeBaron Briggs at Harvard was one of the first in 1891) as a way to relieve presidents of disciplinary responsibilities and begin to guide students in academic and extracurricular matters (Nuss, 2003). The role of college dean expanded to other institutions and began to serve as the institutional conscience and as a guide, supporter, and disciplinarian for students in and out of the classroom. The deans of the late nineteenth and early twentieth centuries took on the responsibility to control and enrich students' experiences outside of class, provide living accommodations and other services, and free the faculty from responsibilities that competed for the time they would otherwise dedicate to their scholarly work. The emergence of this role caused the American Council on Education to call for a conference in April 1937 to discuss what should be done to more purposefully acknowledge and incorporate this trend into higher education systems.

Defining the Purpose and Role of the Dean

The emerging ideas of how students should be treated became the grist for conversation among the nineteen individuals who attended the meeting of the American Council on Education in 1937. After initial discussions, Esther Lloyd-Jones, H. E. Hawks, and L. B. Hopkins drafted a statement, which would eventually be titled the "Student Personnel Point of View" (Roberts, 1998). These individuals came from diverse intellectual and institutional traditions, lending further credence to the importance of the joint statement, which was published in a pamphlet endorsed by the American Council on Education.

The core propositions of the "Student Personnel Point of View" were that students should be viewed holistically, that all students should be encouraged to develop to the full limits of their potential, and that learning should be recognized as the result of a variety of rich experiences that take place both in and outside the classroom. In essence, the document portrayed learning as a process that involves both cognitive and affective abilities and that is stimulated through a variety of experiences. Most important, the document asserted that holistic learning was, and should be, the responsibility of all those in the campus community—faculty, staff, and students. Although the dean was important as a focal point, he or she was not perceived to be either the sole or primary person responsible for this type of engaged learning. The 1937 pamphlet indicated that attention to holism and to engaged learning had been part of collegiate learning from the beginning of colonial education. Student personnel services coordinated by a dean and other staff would help revive this holistic emphasis, but ultimately, faculty, staff, and students still shared the responsibility to fulfill this continuing institutional commitment (American Council on Education, 1937/1984).

The dean and student personnel staff came from a variety of academic preparations and disciplines, among them anthropology, sociology, philosophy, and psychology. Each of these disciplines was tapped for its potential contributions to understanding and enhancing learning. For example, anthropology cultivated a deeper understanding of the meaning and power of culture, and sociology enhanced the understanding of students in their group associations. One of the most influential perspectives was that of educational philosopher John Dewey (1923), whose advocacy for democratic and engaged learning established the core of what the student personnel point of view advocated: active and experiential learning within a learning community of scholars and students.

Student personnel work continued to emerge as an emphasis and had become more important by the end of World War II. However, institutional environments were being shaped by the conditions that dominated the United States after 1945. The United States resisted entering World War II, but when it did, it not only provided the human resources of armies, but also ratcheted up the power of industrialization that had allowed it to grow into an international force. Because of the successful example of the use of industrialization for war, other organizations believed that they could become more efficient and effective if they used similar techniques. The value of expertise and specialization were lauded throughout the military, government, business, and education. Higher education followed suit through increasing bureaucratization. Student personnel began to shift from a shared institutional responsibility to the narrow purview of a defined staff of student personnel workers. This shift was reflected in the revision of the "Student Personnel Point of View" in 1949 (American Council on Education, 1949/1984).

It was only natural that the 1949 statement would reflect the societal conditions present in a postwar environment of industrialism. War veterans returned from service to begin new lives of work, family and the pursuit of prosperity. The resulting baby boom created the demand for more jobs, and expansion of housing, schools, and many other services. Mass production, organization, and bureaucratization were embraced as the only way that these demands could be fulfilled. Higher education adopted similar strategies based on the assumption that specialized functions, addressed by trained individuals with special expertise, would be most effective. In fact, the 1949 statement outlined specific organizational entities that needed to be established, including such areas as admissions, orientation, advising, study skills development, housing, activities, sports and recreation, counseling, religious life, financial management, discipline, and work placement. The statement did not dictate organizational structures to address these functions, but it did propose that there should be specialized individuals or distinct bureaus available to address all these areas and that responsibility in providing the service or function should be clearly defined.

The influence of the 1949 statement was complemented by changes in the broader academic community. All of higher education was becoming more bureaucratic as a result of the sheer numbers of students coming to college. The period from 1945 through the 1970s has been characterized as the Golden Age by those who reflect on the growing prominence and stature of higher education during this time (Thelin, 2003). Faculty size grew exponentially to meet student demand and the academic arena became more and more segmented as a result. New disciplines were established, areas of applied practice became ever more prevalent, and faculty started to focus almost exclusively on students' intellectual needs. Deans and student personnel staffs were all too willing to take on more responsibility for the affairs of students outside of class, and the number of preparation programs for student personnel workers exploded, resulting in the professionalization of a function that was intended to be a shared responsibility.

Professionalization of student personnel work tapped multiple disciplines that could inform the functional responsibilities that each staff member might have. Counselors would be trained in psychology. Housing staff would be trained in management. Program staff would be trained in organizational behavior and leadership. The contributions of these disciplines enhanced the capability and expertise of staff, but the wide range of disciplinary perspectives made it more difficult to keep the core commitments of student personnel work central in everyone's minds.

Specialization, bureaucratization, and professionalization of student personnel work stimulated one additional and very powerful dynamic. The Golden Age of higher education created massive growth in physical facilities, faculty, staff, and programs. This growth required resources. The deans, along with those who now held such titles as director and vice president, controlled administrative areas that were being drawn into institutional competition for larger budgets, staffs, and facilities. These resources, and the power they represented, served only to exaggerate the growing chasm between faculty, with their waning holistic attention to students' experiences, and the student personnel staffs, who were willing to address and work within the emerging gap between student life in class and student life outside the classroom. Ironically, the growing resources that could have been used to enhance institutional effectiveness began to widen the separation between faculty and staff. The emerging bureaucratic and political systems were in place and protected these organizational divisions.

Student Personnel Work as Deeper Teaching

This shift toward specialization and bureaucratization was countered by Esther Lloyd-Jones and Margaret Ruth Smith in *Student*

Personnel Work as Deeper Teaching (1954), a book espousing student personnel work as a catalyst for a return to the holistic treatment of students among all educators.

Esther Lloyd-Jones and Margaret Ruth Smith edited *Student Personnel Work as Deeper Teaching* during a historic period when the focus of student personnel work was shifting to what in retrospect has been recognized as the "student services" era. Interestingly enough, Lloyd-Jones served on both of the American Council on Education committees that drafted the 1937 statement and the 1949 revision. Even though she had been part of the shift advocated in 1949, she quickly saw the dangers inherent in the proposed recommendations.

Lloyd-Jones and Smith's essential proposition was that student personnel work should return to a focus on disseminating and sharing the responsibility for student welfare. They stated, "Student personnel workers should not so much be expert technicians as they should be educators in a somewhat unconventional and new sense. Student personnel workers have many opportunities through their work to contribute to the development of students, to help them learn many lessons and skills of vital importance for their fulfillment as whole persons within a democratic society. Perhaps their most important opportunities are more indirect than direct and exist in their collaborative work with faculty members toward these ends" (p. 12).

Their purpose was not to say that student personnel staffs should be dismantled. The complexity of higher education had become so great that a return to the colonial college of the eighteenth and nineteenth centuries was impossible. However, Lloyd-Jones and Smith offered a warning as well as an alternative way for student personnel work to remain an institutional priority.

Student Personnel Work as Deeper Teaching included chapters by other authors who addressed the various functional areas that had emerged by 1954. Each chapter positioned the service or administrative function in the context of deepening learning. The chapter

"Financial Realities and Resources," by Paul Bulger, effectively illustrates this point. "In order to derive the deeper learning with which this book is concerned, financial aid becomes a counseling process rather than merely a service of appropriating money to students. Its philosophy, policies, and operation must be considered in terms of the individual student, his abilities, needs and hopes, his life in college, his vocational future following graduation, and how such assistance may contribute to his development" (Lloyd-Jones & Smith, 1954, p. 225).

The fact that these authors asserted in 1954 that financial aid should be informed by counseling and development perspectives is ironic when contemporary circumstances are adding greater debt burden to students' lives, without providing much assistance in determining if and how students might begin to manage their debt.

Lloyd-Jones, Smith, and their colleagues urged campuses to approach student personnel work as a catalyst in the college or university, a broker of experience, and an integrator of students' various educational endeavors. They proposed five conditions that would indicate that a campus demonstrated a commitment to deepening learning:

- Student personnel workers and teachers would work together as educators to accomplish common objectives.

- Cooperative programs by faculty, student personnel workers, and students would be designed to improve the campus communities in which they shared membership; programs would be centered in the small, natural communities of the campus.

- "Deeper learning" would be emphasized by both students and staff; group life and conditions for growth for all students would be improved through consultation among all those affected.

- Participation and cooperation would be expected.

- There would be a concern for the quality of human relations in the community.

These conditions were straightforward and challenging. They were relevant in 1954, and they may be even more relevant today. The reality is that the student services focus continued to dominate during most of the 1950s and 1960s. Even when the student services era (which emphasized the creation of a functional area for each aspect of the college experience) yielded to the student development movement of the 1970s and beyond (which emphasized the exploration of ways to help students achieve personal, intellectual, and social growth), the distinct and organizationally cloistered emphasis of student personnel work never returned to the idea of student personnel work as a shared responsibility as advocated by Lloyd-Jones and Smith.

The compelling relevance of deeper teaching has been more recently advocated in the ideas and principles of several national studies and think-tank papers. Although these statements have not explicitly acknowledged derivation from the core ideas of *Student Personnel Work as Deeper Teaching*, it doesn't take much to see their symmetry. Nancy Evans and Robert Reason (2001) analyzed thirteen different statements from 1937 through 1999 for consistency of themes and focus. Nine of the twelve themes in their model are broadly endorsed in all. These themes include commitment to a holistic perspective, attention to individual differences, student agency, interactionist perspective, consideration of context, intentionality, empirically grounded initiatives, a role in instruction and learning, and collaboration (p. 371). Kari Taylor (2005) conducted an analysis of historical and more recent statements about enhancing learning. She proposed the three themes of "creating learning environments that facilitate the positive growth of natural communities, constructing curricula from experiential education opportunities, and basing pedagogy on challenge-and-support principles" (p. 18) as the consistent core of the statements she reviewed.

These models are more than best guesses for exemplary practice. They are based on, and reinforced by, a long succession of empirical studies that substantiate the importance and potential for deepening students' learning experiences. Alexander Astin's ongoing research (1993, 1999) through the Cooperative Institutional Research Program has repeatedly documented that student learning is the result of students' being engaged more intensely through experiences both in and outside the classroom. George Kuh and his colleagues (2005) studied twenty colleges and universities that were successful in creating environments that contribute to student success. This analysis identified a number of conditions that are part of common understanding or represent promising new practices, all of which document the importance of creating campus cultures of high expectation, intense engagement, and shared responsibility for deep learning. Marcia Baxter Magolda (2004) created the Learning Partnerships Model from the qualitative study of students' progressive experience during and after college. This model includes elements of support (validating learners' capacity to know, situating learning in students' experiences, and defining learning as mutually constructing meaning) and challenge (portraying knowledge as complex and socially constructed, reinforcing that self is central to knowledge construction, and sharing authority and expertise) that enhance learning. The evidence that deeper learning is possible when institutions set their collective minds to the task is significant and unequivocal.

We now know that a large body of research related to the importance of deepening student learning confirms Lloyd-Jones and Smith's assertions in 1954, which leads to the inevitable question of why *Student Personnel Work as Deeper Teaching* was not embraced more actively. On a personal note, I struggled with this question for some time. I was stunned and relieved of much of my discomfort when I read Thomas Ehrlich's "Dewey Versus Hutchins: The Next Round" (1997). Ehrlich describes the great and historic debate that began in 1936 between John Dewey, the advocate of engaged and democratic learning, and Robert Maynard Hutchins, young president of the University of Chicago and an advocate for the "great books" approach to learning. Dewey believed that learning was most useful and influential when students were immersed in their studies and in their communities of learning and practice. "Learning starts with problems rooted in experiences, Dewey urged, and continues with the application of increasingly complex ideas and increasingly sophisticated skills to increasingly complicated problems" (p. 226). By contrast, Hutchins believed that liberal education should be based on reading the works of the great thinkers in order to understand them on their own merit, rather than attempting to see them applied in students' experiences. Ehrlich concluded that Hutchins's view of learning had a profound, if not victorious, impact on higher education through much of the twentieth century. However, Ehrlich went on to propose that the balance between detached and intellectualized learning versus learning that is informed by the needs of students and connected to their experience may actually be shifting. He provided examples indicating that the type of learning advocated by Dewey is gaining momentum; community-service learning, problem-based learning, collaborative learning, and interactive technologies are all examples of the kind of pedagogical approaches that are increasingly prominent among best practices that enhance students' learning.

Ehrlich's description of the struggle between Dewey and Hutchins provided a plausible explanation for why Lloyd-Jones and Smith's advocacy for deeper learning was not embraced in 1954. The original propositions of the "Student Personnel Point of View" (1937/1984) and Lloyd-Jones and Smith's reiteration and further explanation in *Student Personnel Work as Deeper Teaching* were substantially based on Dewey's views of democratic education. As such, the 1937 and 1954 proposals were increasingly marginalized as the twentieth century continued to embrace the educational models of Hutchins and others who saw education as "the single-minded pursuit of intellectual virtues" (p. 228). The political conditions that existed among key leaders in the emerging field of student personnel work may also have diminished the impact of Lloyd-Jones and Smith's work. Women's voices were frequently, if not consistently, marginalized in the educational environment of the 1950s and 1960s. The focus and inertia of complex organizations and systems may have been a third cause for Lloyd-Jones and Smith's ideas falling on deaf ears, especially when so much was at stake among those who benefited from keeping the systems as they were. If Ehrlich is correct in his analysis, which is also the thesis of this chapter, then a return to a focus on deeper learning and the exploration of new and innovative ways to foster it will become more prevalent across the landscape of higher education in the years to come.

Ehrlich's analysis helps explain what might have contributed to the shift in views on learning and how student personnel work (now more frequently known as student affairs) should be pursued. In addition, considerable research on the impact of higher education, new models for collegiate institutions, and our experience all point to the importance of reconnecting notions that have become dichotomous in contemporary education: cognitive and emotional intelligence, theory and practice, reflecting and acting. Numerous models for enhancing learning have been proposed that may help higher education begin to seal these fissures.

Deeper Learning and Its Relationship to Leadership

As you will see in Chapter Two, the explicit focus on leadership through curricular or cocurricular means is a relatively new phenomenon. The expanded interest that we presently see has given rise to many programs, most conceived in very idiosyncratic ways. The rise in the number of such organizations as the International Leadership Association, and the enhanced focus on leadership in many others are clear indicators that the topic is of interest throughout higher education. Yet it is difficult to document and substantiate the importance of these programs, and it is even more challenging to demonstrate that there is a deep and lasting impact in students' and graduates' lives. If evidence of the deep impact of leadership learning were available, we would probably all know it and would be seeking to replicate it.

I propose that deeper learning and deeper leadership are closely aligned, if not one and the same. Leadership capability is an important outcome of the higher education experience, but it is not the only or necessarily the most desirable outcome. As we look ever more closely at what we are achieving, there is emerging evidence that deeper learning is a necessary condition to foster deeper leadership. This relationship was proposed in *Leadership Reconsidered: Engaging Higher Education in Social Change* (Astin & Astin, 2000). How might learning be defined in order to make the important connection between learning and leadership clear and explicit? In relatively simple language, relying on both historical and contemporary views, and informed by our most compelling learning experiences, deeper learning might then be defined as a commitment to foster a level of learning that pushes us so deeply into our own questions that the conclusions are unforgettable.

If deeper learning in leadership is a goal, colleges and universities will need to explore the mental models that dominate the organizational structures, processes, and pedagogies that they use to foster learning. Such models as the "Student Learning Imperative" (ACPA, 1994), "Powerful Partnerships" (American Association of Higher Education, American College Personnel Association, & National Association of Student Personnel Administrators, 1998), and "Learning Reconsidered" (National Association of Student Personnel Administrators & American College Personnel Association, 2004) all call for fundamental renovation of our approaches. These reports consistently indicate that deeper learning will require a return to a holistic focus on students and their experiences.

One more model that has emerged on the contemporary landscape is the one proposed in the *Greater Expectations* report (Association of American Colleges and Universities, 2002). Along with reinforcing many of the themes noted in other reports, this one additionally proposes that many voices must be heard in order to construct the institutions and learning processes that will help higher education fulfill its mission in the modern day. Responsible scholarship should include among these voices the influential educators and organizations that have provided important research, models, and theory over the years. In addition, a commitment to including many voices should embrace all those in the academy who can contribute positively to learning. Faculty are central to our institutions of higher learning, but research evidence underscores the importance of broadening the conversation about learning and leadership to include student affairs staff, other college or university staff, and most important, students themselves.

The models on which higher education has organized itself emerged over time and have been influenced by historical contexts that may no longer be relevant. Therefore, we will have to undertake a careful examination of the roles played by faculty, staff, and students, and of how these might be more purposefully aligned with the goals of enhancing learning and leadership. Moving beyond conventional models is at the heart of innovating for a more successful future, and this innovation can be best achieved by including recommendations from students, faculty, staff, community members, and other stakeholders. By sharing responsibility among all concerned, we have the potential to create the kind of campus cultures that enhance learning and leadership for everyone.

2

Context of Leadership Learning

Most of us involved in developing leadership are all too familiar with the dynamics of the following exchange. After the first blush of excitement about hearing new ideas—"Hmm, sounds interesting" and "Great idea!"—there is almost always someone else who says, "Wait a minute. Leadership comes naturally. You either have it or you don't. Those who do have it hone their skills as a natural part of going to college. Why would we want to devote precious resources to nurturing leadership if students will become leaders regardless of our efforts?" Such a statement might compel another to respond, "Plus, don't leadership programs merely perpetuate the privilege of those who have had the most opportunity? What about the students who are on the margin and can never gain access to these kinds of things?" Such a mix of perspectives will stimulate a lively discussion of what defines leadership, whether and how it can be developed, and what role higher education might play in fostering it.

This chapter explores the context of leadership development and provides ideas for responding to comments similar to those I've just described. We need to be prepared for discussions about leadership learning, and we need to be open to points of view that are as diverse as the participants. Just as our favorite foods are the result of diverse and interesting ingredients, the resources and ideas we contribute and the new ones we encounter as we engage with our colleagues are, likewise, ingredients. Some cooking ingredients disappear into the amalgam of flavors, whereas others remain distinguishable once the dish is prepared. Similarly, certain ideas disappear into the complex flavors and textures, and others remain distinct and become the defining essence of what we accomplish together. If we don't prepare for conversations about leadership, we run the risk of failing to advocate for ideas we hold dear. A complex and interesting mix of ideas will receive a welcome response in most higher education environments. When the focus is on how to enhance student learning, the key is finding issues that elicit contributions from a variety of stakeholders. These face-to-face encounters help everyone see that we value the same things and seek to shape our learning communities in ways that will respond more effectively to modern challenges.

This chapter is a resource to prepare you to explore leadership issues with your colleagues. I will begin with a brief background on how leadership has been viewed and addressed over time and then discuss how this relative newcomer to the academy has grown in the last fifty years, both as an area of academic inquiry and as part of students' experience. Finally, I will suggest ways in which leadership learning can enhance the overall collegiate experience.

The Study of Leadership

Throughout history, numerous authors have explicitly or implicitly explored leadership in their writing, and some in their own life experiences. We have been given a rich literature—historical accounts, biographies, proposals for social change—through which to ponder leading and leadership.

Barbara Kellerman (2001) has suggested a reading list of ten classic texts for all those who seek to understand leadership. These include pieces that analyze the essence of leadership (Machiavelli's *The Prince*; Carlyle's *On Heroes, Hero-Worship, and the Heroic in History*; Freud's three books, *Group Psychology and the Analysis of the Ego, Civilization and Its Discontents*, and *Moses and Monotheism*; Arendt's *The Origins of Totalitarianism*; Barnard's *The Functions of the Executive*) and others that illustrate leadership through the authors' personal experiences (Hamilton, Madison, and Jay's *The Federalist Papers*; King's "Letter from Birmingham Jail"; Freidan's

The Feminine Mystique). Together, these ten works reflect the breadth of inquiry about leadership throughout history and demonstrate the critical importance of context when analyzing leadership. Surely we each have our own favorite texts, but Kellerman's recommendations would likely make most of our short lists. Following are a few examples from these ten classic works.

Although readers can take away many lessons from Niccolo Machiavelli's *The Prince* (1513/1954), Kellerman observes that one of Machiavelli's most important assertions is that leadership can be taught or cultivated. Machiavelli's ideas were radical in a time when monarchies dominated the political and economic landscapes and when only those with specific backgrounds and experiences were deemed worthy of governing. What about notions of leader privilege in more contemporary circumstances? When asked why they believe they are good candidates for leadership opportunities, many interested college students offer a very simple answer: "I was born this way." Machiavelli's analyses of the human condition and proposals for how one might respond to the call to leadership provide clear evidence that leadership can and should be cultivated.

In *The Origins of Totalitarianism* (1949), Hannah Arendt opens another critical issue: Can leadership actually be bad? Of course, if we are completely honest, we know that it can be, but many of us attempt to deny bad leadership by saying that destructive leaders exhibit something other than leadership. Arendt's powerful assertion forces us to be careful about what we do, and demands that we think seriously about how to ensure that the leaders we nurture will serve others and enhance the human condition. Arendt also states that leaders and followers are interdependent; leaders depend on acquiescence, and followers seek hope and purpose. When followers lack the fortitude to think carefully, to confront abuse, and to be diligent in their advocacy for others, they set the stage (sometimes unintentionally) for destructive individuals to take control and thus create potentially dangerous conditions.

Almost as if in response to Arendt, Martin Luther King Jr.'s "Letter from Birmingham Jail" (1964) is an act of leadership that confronts injustice. In the swirling center of the civil rights movement, King knew that making a difference meant going to one of the hotbeds of abuse: Birmingham, Alabama. There, he advocated a different way of speaking truth to authority: nonviolent resistance. Responding to white clergymen's admonitions to blacks to end their protests, King couched his letter in the cultural language they could most easily understand—the language of the Bible, of philosophy and justice. King penned "Letter from Birmingham Jail" in a squalid, dark, and dehumanizing place, which brings to mind stories of other great leaders of social change, such as Mahatma Gandhi and Nelson Mandela. The lesson to be learned from these accounts is that, at minimum, voluntary or imposed retreat spurs breakthrough thinking and facilitates discovery of purpose and that, in extraordinary cases, isolation and deprivation can produce profoundly influential leadership.

Machiavelli, Arendt, and King teach us that leadership can be learned, that leaders can be bad, that following makes us complicitous with our leaders, and that leadership is frequently a result of conviction borne of deep reflection. Kellerman's top ten required reading list holds many other valuable insights as well, and her analyses highlight the eloquent and insightful sources that are readily available to us and relatively well known among broad segments of society. In addition to the historic and classic analyses of leadership, contemporary educators continue to debate the meaning and nuance of leadership.

A recent exchange of messages over the listserv of the International Leadership Association revealed 62 books that qualified for the "top 50 list of most influential books in leadership" (Harter, 2005). The original message that resulted in this compilation simply asked the approximately one thousand members to offer their recommendations on the best books on leadership. The list of favorites (which appears at the end of this chapter) is eclectic and covers a broad array of leadership environments, dilemmas, and possibilities. The sheer number of books nominated attests to the range of literature available to the serious student.

The available number of essays, articles, and books about leadership challenges the reader to be both discerning as well as integrative. Discernment requires reading with a critical eye, engaging in analysis, and constantly applying models and theory to practice. Some books are very detailed and rigorous in intellectual content but break down in their applicability to experience. Other books are based on no research at all but propose perspectives that are very useful and apply in numerous environments. Still others are "airplane reading" that may have come from a writer who was deeply informed through research and practice but who simply wanted to write something with popular appeal. My experience is that the length, the density, the reference list, and other indicators can help in discerning useful books from the trite and trivial, but it is important to remember that thorough and expertly researched books can come in very pedestrian trappings.

Having determined which literature is valuable, the reader must then integrate the relationships, connections, or contradictions among the various models of leading and leadership. Various authors posed their ways of making sense of the emerging research in psychology in a special edition of the *American Psychologist* (American Psychological Association, 2007). One well-respected and often replicated model (Komives, Lucas, & McMahon, 1998, 2007) suggests that the prevailing understanding of leadership has evolved dramatically over time. The Great Man perspective (mid-1800s to early 1900s) proposed that leaders were born or emerged as a result of Darwinist dynamics that allowed only those with natural abilities to survive in such a role. The trait period that followed (1907–1947) contended that there were certain traits that differentiated leaders from those who were not. The behavioral period (1950s to early 1980s) advocated that there was one best way to lead and that to be effective required combining relational and task dimensions in leadership. The situational and contingency perspectives (1950s to 1960s) proposed that leadership style should differ based on specific environmental factors. Influence models (mid-1920s to 1977) evolved to analyze more deeply the influence and exchange that took place among leaders and followers. The reciprocal models (1978 to the present) have asserted that leadership is a shared relationship between leaders and followers. Finally, chaos and systems models (1990 to the present) seek to describe the dynamics of leadership in a rapidly changing world where control is unrealistic and interacting systems regularly impact on each other. Chapter Three will provide summaries of the most widely used theories at present, and Chapter Four offers newer models that are just beginning to gain acceptance and use.

The frameworks of understanding leadership expressed by Kellerman (2001) and Komives et al. (1998, 2007) call attention to the variety of assumptions about leadership present in our consciousness. In some cases, numerous ideas converge into one context, pointing leaders in many different directions. Roberts (2003) recounted a particularly illustrative example of the reality and difficulty of multiple leadership models thriving in one collegiate environment. A team of consultants was enlisted to visit a select, liberal arts institution in North America with the intent of determining the best strategy for designing a leadership program. Through interviews, document analyses, and observation, the consultants collected much useful information. The most stunning realization, which came after two days of intense interaction, was that the students, faculty, and staff had widely divergent opinions about what constituted leadership and how it could be nurtured as part of the collegiate experience. In particular, the team of consultants identified four models at work: (1) leaders are born, not made, (2) leadership capability is a natural and assumed outcome of the learning experience, (3) leadership understanding and capability result from deliberate and focused education and critical examination, and (4) leadership understanding and capability emerge from acts of service and involvement and can best be understood through these experiences. These four models were not recognized prior to the consultation, yet the individuals who held these different views had great potential influence over the success of the new leadership program. The biggest challenge facing the students, faculty, and staff was to identify and acknowledge their differences as they worked toward a consensus that ultimately resulted in a stronger, more effective model.

The most comprehensive collection of leadership articles and perspectives can be found in *Encyclopedia of Leadership* (Goethals, Sorenson, & Burns, 2004). Its four volumes, almost two thousand pages, and 309 contributors attest to the interest in leadership over time and across the various disciplines that define the academy. Although these authors propose that leadership studies may have merit as a discipline in itself, they also extol the virtue of leadership studies in enhancing other disciplines. The question of disciplinarity itself is an important point in the evolution of leadership thought.

The intellectual components of higher education are divided into disciplines, each of which has stood the tests of credibility and longevity—the criteria—that serve as the gatekeepers of legitimacy. Recognized disciplines with track records of rigor, scientific analysis, and general applicability reign supreme in the academy, and anyone who would attempt to deny this in most institutions in the early twenty-first century is naive. Although some authors in leadership studies would assert disciplinary status, many would not. Beyond the leadership studies ranks, few faculty would agree that leadership is even close to a discipline at this time. The struggle over this question has been under way for many years and is likely to continue. Perhaps William Howe (2005) says it best:

> I see "leadership studies" or "organizational leadership" or similar phrases for the endeavor (perhaps those in themselves can be differentiated?) as marking off a "field" but by no means marking off a distinct "discipline." There are people, I realize, who want to make it a discipline, though I think that is a mistake that would

delimit and constrain what is a growing and multi-disciplinary concern that includes research, education, and practice, and that should draw from the social sciences, the humanities, the arts, and the professions. The desire to make the area into a discipline is, as I see it, a desire to garner increased legitimacy, but I fear such a desire will do more harm than good to an <u>area that is still in its adolescence and that needs to remain open</u> and permeable, at least at this point in its evolution. Furthermore, I suspect that the academy will always be reluctant to grant any kind of full-fledged disciplinary status to "leadership," primarily because the very word embeds—despite many efforts, mine included, to democratize it today—an ineradicable elitism that is anathema to most scholars and educators.

Persuasive as Howe's perspective may be, many readers of this book and others who invest much intellectual and personal energy in understanding and practicing leadership are likely to hold a different perspective. They would assert that the increasing number of models and theories of leadership add to the potential legitimacy of leadership studies. The dilemma of this evolution might be explained by using Thomas Kuhn's analysis of paradigm shifts and the rise of professions. "In the absence of a paradigm or some candidate for paradigm, all of the facts that could possibly pertain to the development of a given science are likely to seem equally relevant. As a result, early fact-gathering is a far more nearly random activity than the one that subsequent scientific development makes familiar" (1970, p. 15). The shifts in leadership understanding over time contribute to the impression that all are equally relevant, creating confusion regarding which theories might be more helpful and appropriate than others.

The credibility of leadership studies as a discipline or interdisciplinary field took a major stride forward when James MacGregor

Burns called for a conference of leadership scholars. Although the conference did not conclude with a general theory, the result of the thought-provoking meetings is a rich collection of perspectives on leadership. *The Quest for a General Theory of Leadership* (GTOL) (Goethals & Sorenson, 2006) documents these scholars' processes of discovery and includes summaries and integrations of many of the key and sometimes opposing perspectives on leadership. Summarizing the group's process, J. Thomas Wren wrote that the efforts of the GTOL group are "merely intended as the prologue for a continuing discourse concerning the integration of the varied understandings of leadership" (p. 34). Burns concluded that "we now see leadership as an influence process, both visible and invisible, in a society inherited, constructed, and perceived as the interaction of persons in human (and inhuman) conditions of inequality—an interaction measured by ethical and moral values and by the degree of realization of intended, comprehensive, and durable change" (p. 239).

Whether it is a concentration, field, discipline, or interdisciplinary discourse, leadership studies has a long and interesting history. The introduction provided here reflects only a context, a partial one at that, for the many resources that the true student of leadership will want to explore. From this context of the inquiry about leadership, we turn to the question of how leadership capacity might be enhanced as both an individual and collective phenomenon.

Developing Leadership

Chapter One offered background on how student personnel work, or as it is more often called today, student affairs or development, was established at the turn of the twentieth century. The central objectives of the student personnel movement were to advocate that students should be viewed holistically, that they should be encouraged to develop to their fullest potential, and that learning should be recognized as the result of a variety of rich experiences that take place both inside and outside of the classroom environment. Residential and other groups that students joined for athletic, creative, social, and other purposes were seen as natural communities in which students would apply knowledge beyond the classroom and, perhaps more important, were recognized as the testing grounds for group and leadership behavior. These are the core premises on which much of student affairs work is based. The commitment to fostering leadership was explicitly named as one of the values of this work (Roberts, 1988), but an intentional focus on leadership did not emerge until much later in the evolution of the field. Even the goal of preserving democracy for future generations, which drew great attention following World War II, did not spawn programs designed to develop leadership potential in students.

However, the 1960s and 1970s were a different matter. This Golden Age of higher education witnessed mushrooming enrollments and expanding institutions as the result of the baby boom following the end of World War II. As the early "boomers" came of age, colleges and universities threw open their doors to welcome the largest and most diverse student population that higher education had ever witnessed. This expansion brought with it a number of interesting challenges.

There are many interpretations of why the 1960s marked a turning point for U.S. higher education. Some say that the shadow of World Wars I and II created the silent 1950s, characterized by families withdrawing into privacy and enjoying greater job opportunity, secure in the knowledge that democracy had been saved. Patriotism ran high as memories of the war faded and the scars they created healed. Even a brief study of the emerging mass media of the 1950s reveals many idealized and conformist perspectives of the way things should be. *Father Knows Best, Leave It to Beaver, The Adventures of Ozzie and Harriet,* and other television and radio programs portrayed American families and American life in very prescriptive ways. The irony is that the seeds of the 1960s may have been sown during this idealized time, seeds germinating into challenging questions about sweeping social and civil rights issues. Questions about whether conformity and uniformity were best. Questions about the equality of opportunity for all people, especially when many were beginning to see the evidence of inequity for women and people of color.

The social awakening that unfolded in the 1960s and 1970s might have occurred on its own, but this awakening had a greater impact because of the sheer number of young people coming of age at the time. The number and diversity of voices were so large that they could not be contained. Students who had previously behaved in conventional ways became agents of change on their campuses and elsewhere. Examples of the dramatic impact of activism in students' lives include the Mississippi Freedom Summer of 1964, when college students went into the south to register black voters as part of the civil rights movement; the antiwar movement against the Vietnam War; the women's movement; and the rise in environmentalism. This period of awakening may have given birth to questions about how best to foster and shape leadership potential in students. Student affairs staff at a number of colleges and universities began to provide conferences and other experiences to bring students together around issues of leadership. Some of those who were students in the early 1970s knew that they had only survived their experiences as undergraduate student leaders rather than learned much from them. Informed by their own experience, many of those who would serve as young staff in student affairs divisions in the middle to late 1970s would bring a perspective that students should have the opportunity to learn more about leadership than they had themselves.

Another influence during this period was the cry for relevance in learning. The teaching-centered pedagogies that dominated most colleges and universities seemed abstract and aloof to many students. With the introduction of applied methods, current topics courses, and even new forms of out-of-class engagement such as "teach-ins" came a push to transform learning. Students were challenging higher education to reexamine its role in preparing young people for service to society and the American industrial giant, and to incorporate social, environmental, and political concerns into general education. The "agenda" for learning was up for grabs, and many institutions withdrew from prescriptive education and increasingly left it to students to decide which educational programs were most beneficial.

Within the context of the 1960s and 1970s, it comes as no great wonder that educators began to take greater interest in how to foster more informed leaders who could be part of governmental, business, education, and societal change. Kuhn's analysis of changes in theoretical paradigms may apply equally well to changes in educational programs: "The novel theory seems a direct response to crisis" (1970, p. 75).

The First Programs

Although the Center for Creative Leadership (Glover & Wilson, 2006) did not emerge on a college or university campus, it influenced the inception of leadership as an academic area as well as the cocurricular emphasis that will be described later. Established in 1970 to address the needs of business leaders, the Center eventually broadened its mission to include not-for-profit, educational, and other organizations. The name of the Center conveyed its core belief that creativity was essential to leadership during times of change. The Center for Creative Leadership was one of the first organizations to challenge conventional assumptions about leading and leadership (such as "leaders are born, not made"), and it focused heavily on personal development as a key ingredient in augmenting leadership potential.

Although it is difficult to pinpoint the origin of collegiate leadership programs, the President's Leadership Class at the University of Colorado was likely one, if not the first, of the major systematic efforts to foster leadership in students. This 1972 initiative arose out of concern for the difficult dynamics of the day and a belief that young people should be encouraged to engage positively in their communities, becoming leaders in school and eventually in their work environments. Initiated and funded by private business, this university-community partnership attracted the most talented high school graduates from across Colorado. Students were offered scholarships and an invitation to participate in a special academic program focused on leadership. A second program, which began in 1976 at the University of Maryland, combined curricular and cocurricular programs guided by a peer team called the Leadership Development Program Team. Internships, courses, conferences, a resource center, and one of the first cocurricular transcripts came out of this program.

As these new programs sprang up, campuses began to compare what they were doing. In the spring of 1976, the American College Personnel Association's Commission IV established a Leadership Development Task Force to survey campuses on the ways in which they were fostering leadership. The task force compiled resources from all campuses that were known to have programs related to leadership, resulting in the source of information for the comprehensive model that the task force later detailed in *Student Leadership Programs in Higher Education* (Roberts, 1981). This model implored campuses to approach leadership work by creating comprehensive opportunities for students that addressed diverse populations through multiple strategies and strove to achieve the combined purposes of training, education, and development. The task force sponsored regional workshops in order to continue the dialogue about best practices in leadership programs. The work of the original task force eventually turned into an interassociation effort and contributed to the creation of standards for student leadership programs adopted by the Council for the Advancement of Standards (CAS) in 1996.

Many other initiatives occurred during this time and contributed to the virtual explosion of interest in leadership during the 1980s and 1990s. Burns's *Leadership,* published in 1978, stimulated the exploration of leadership as a transformational process in organizations. Conferences, among them the Campus Opportunity Outreach League in 1984 and Campus Compact in 1985, were established to serve specific college populations such as women student leaders and black student leaders as well as to encourage community service. A number of philanthropic foundations also became interested in leadership. Among the first was the Luce Foundation, which sponsored the Association of American College's (AAC) conferences in the late 1980s on the study and practice of leadership. The Kellogg Foundation joined later with grants to thirty-one campuses and organizations to establish leadership programs in the 1990s. Of course, throughout this time some of the most influential books were published on leadership, including Kouzes and Posner's *The Leadership Challenge* (1987); Gardner's *On Leadership* (1990); Rost's *Leadership for the Twenty-First Century* (1991); Heifetz's *Leadership Without Easy Answers* (1994); Wren's *The Leader's Companion* (1995); and Komives, Lucas, and McMahon's *Exploring Leadership: For College Students Who Want to Make a Difference* (1998).

It is significant that throughout the 1980s and 1990s there were both conferences targeted primarily for student affairs staff working in cocurricular programs as well as academic conferences targeted to faculty who were writing and theorizing about leadership. Some of these conferences involved overlapping populations, and these were, in many instances, the ones of greatest interest. Such conferences allowed staff and faculty the opportunity to hear each other's viewpoints, frequently resulting in the subtle or not-so-subtle tension between students' classroom and extracurricular activities that I described in Chapter One. There were even isolated examples where committees were established to draft statements that articulated the importance of joint work between faculty and staff. Unfortunately, the research to substantiate the critical importance of academic and student affairs collaboration had not yet emerged; had this research been available, there may have been more of a commitment to sustain these efforts. One of the efforts to draft a joint statement came as early as the AAC conferences in the late 1980s; however, the participants could not agree on how collaboration would proceed or on a shared vision of what they sought to achieve.

Leadership development has been an implicit commitment of higher education in the United States since the inception of colonial colleges. Beginning in the 1970s, colleges paid more explicit attention to the issue, particularly by establishing special programs to address questions of leadership. However, leadership programs available outside of class and the emergence of the research and study of leadership in class developed in distinct and separate ways. How to respond to that reality is the topic to which we now turn.

The Joint Work of Leadership Learning

Thus far, we've explored how those who research and theorize about leadership and those who seek to engage students and develop leadership potential have pursued their work independent of one other. But there is a fine line between theory and practice, and there have always been those who crossed the boundaries. Warren Bennis (O'Toole, 2005) is one person considered to have walked the path of theory and practice throughout his career in education. John Gardner (1990) is another who sought to relate theories of leadership to the reality of private sector work. Nevertheless, the evidence is all too persuasive that the study and practice of leadership are frequently approached separately. This is especially prevalent on campuses where there are hard and fast distinctions between the preparation, roles, and perspectives of faculty and student affairs staff. The real challenge for those who value leadership is to bring these necessary and complementary processes together.

Laura Osteen (2005) has proposed that, as leadership educators inside and outside of class, faculty and staff need to find a new language that describes these potentially joint efforts. She advocates that we call this "leadership learning," a term that reflects both the content of leadership studies as well as the process of helping students explore and develop the capacity to lead. Leadership learning reflects the potential for continuous discovery through the interplay of theory and practice.

The Opportunity of Collaboration

In order to establish the respectful and mutually beneficial conditions under which leadership learning can be pursued, it's important to consider what models of working together might be effective. One term that seems to be gaining great popularity on some campuses is the word *collaboration*. This is a term that may have lost much of its transformative potential because some use it without a clear understanding of its true meaning. The word collaboration is mistakenly used as if it encompassed various degrees of partnerships such as noncompetition, accommodation, sponsorship, and cooperation. Although these other terms have value in themselves, they do not carry the implications of collaboration. Collaboration means to labor together, to join in mutual endeavor and common purpose. In order to achieve what is possible in leadership learning, it seems that an understanding and a willingness to truly collaborate is critical. Peter Magolda (2005) raised important questions to explore when determining if collaboration might be useful, and observed that success in doing so depended on establishing meaningful, reciprocal and responsive relationships.

Larraine Matusak (2005) proposed seven principles of collaboration that were derived from earlier work by Kellogg Leadership Studies Project participants. These seven principles included: to promote a collective leadership process, to structure a learning environment, to support relationships and interconnectedness, to foster shared power, practice stewardship and service, to value diversity and inclusiveness, and to commit to self-development. If these principles were adopted, imagine how different the conversations would be when people with diverse perspectives and voices discussed how to advance the study and practice of leadership.

Although I do not presume to characterize all college and university environments, I speak to all too many faculty and staff alike who experience life on campus as a struggle for power, resources, and prestige. The irony of this is that, when drawn together in an off-campus setting, faculty and student affairs staff frequently find much to affirm about each other and are able to engage in respectful discourse around important leadership topics. One example of this phenomenon is the International Leadership Association, a relatively young association that seeks to improve the quality of leadership worldwide by inviting participants who study and practice leadership in business, education, politics, and other areas of service to work together. This ambitious, perhaps even audacious, vision requires an adaptive and responsive commitment on the part of all its members. When individuals and groups recognize that they cannot independently achieve an important goal, amazing things happen, including the destruction of barriers that might have become insurmountable under other circumstances.

If a serious commitment to collaboration and mutual work were adopted, a number of new and provocative questions could enter the conversation. Leadership educators could begin to explore how this special field could foster the depth of engagement that is necessary for higher education to be most effective. Leadership educators could also create ways to connect leadership learning with students' interests and commitments to social change and the improvement of the human condition. Because the study of leadership is so dependent on many disciplines and perspectives, exciting possibilities arise—for example, could leadership educators actually help refine or create new models for the generation and integration of knowledge in the academy? Ultimately, could leadership educators begin to work together to ensure the institutionalization of leadership studies and development and thereby avoid its being dismissed as just another fad, as so many other great ideas have been?

These questions, challenges, and opportunities reflect at least a starting point for the mutual work of those who are passionate in their commitment to advance leadership. Leadership studies faculty on campus often feel marginalized by their academic colleagues because of questions about disciplinary credibility and position in the institution. Student affairs staff are also subject to marginalization because they represent such a small proportion of faculty and staff and are frequently characterized as involved only in service or administrative matters. These two groups, and probably others, could benefit from joining together to demonstrate new ways to advance learning. Leadership learning could become a catalyst and role model for changes in other academic areas of the college or university where true collaborative work would be helpful. Such joint efforts between faculty and staff could demonstrate the power of curricular and cocurricular engagement that is likely to transform the quality of learning in collegiate education in the future.

Most Influential Books on Leadership

Adler, N. (1996). *International dimensions of organizational behavior* (3rd ed.). Belmont, CA: Wadsworth.

Argyris, C. (1964). *Integrating the individual and the organization.* New York: Wiley.

Argyris, C. (1993). *Knowledge for action.* San Francisco: Jossey-Bass.

Bandura, A. (1985). *Social foundations of thought and action.* Englewood Cliffs, NJ: Prentice Hall.

Barker, R. (2002). *On the nature of leadership.* Lanham, MD: University Press of America.

Bass, B. (1990). *Bass & Stogdill's handbook of leadership.* New York: Free Press.

Bass, B., & Avolio, B. (1985). *Leadership and performance beyond expectations*. Thousand Oaks, CA: Sage.

Beck, D., & Cowan, C. (1996). *Spiral dynamics*. Oxford: Blackwell Business.

Bennis, W., & Nanus, B. (2003). *Leaders* (2nd ed.). New York: Collins.

Block, P. (1996). *Stewardship*. San Francisco: Berrett-Koehler.

Bohm, D. (1992). *Thought as a system*. New York: Routledge.

Bradford, D., & Cohen, A. (1998). *Power up: Transforming organizations through shared leadership*. New York: Wiley.

Burchard, B. (2003). *The student leadership guide*. San Francisco: swift-Kick Development.

Burns, J. M. (1978). *Leadership*. New York: Harper Perennial.

Cawthon, D. (2002). *Philosophical foundations of leadership*. New Brunswick, NJ: Transaction.

Chaleff, I. (1995). *The courageous follower*. San Francisco: Berrett-Koehler.

Chemers, M., & Ayman, R. (1993). *Leadership theory and research*. Orlando, FL: Academic Press.

Clark, D. B. (2000). *To lead the way: A fantasy journey into leadership development*. San Jose, CA: Writers Club Press.

Conger, J. (1989). *The charismatic leader*. San Francisco: Jossey-Bass.

Covey, S. (1992). *Principle centered leadership*. New York: Free Press.

Covey, S. (2004). *The 8th habit*. New York: Free Press.

Drath, W. (2001). *The deep blue sea*. San Francisco: Jossey-Bass.

Fiedler, F. (1967). *A theory of leadership effectiveness*. New York: McGraw-Hill.

Fiedler, F., & Garcia, J. (1987). *New approaches to effective leadership*. New York: Wiley.

Foster, W. (1986). *Paradigms and promises*. Amherst, NY: Prometheus.

Foster, W. (2001). *The reconstruction of leadership*. New York: Hyperion.

Frieberg, K., & Frieberg, J. (1996). *NUTS! Southwest Airlines' crazy recipe for business and personal success*. New York: Bard Books.

Fulmer, R. (2001). *The leadership investment*. New York: American Management Association.

Gardner, J. (1990). *On leadership*. New York: Free Press.

Gerber, R. (2003). *Leadership the Eleanor Roosevelt way*. New York: Portfolio Trade.

Greenleaf, R. K., & Spears, L. C. (2002). *Servant leadership: A journey into the nature of legitimate power and greatness* (25th anniversary ed.). New York: Paulist Press.

Hackman, M., & Johnson, C. (2003). *Leadership: A communication perspective* (4th ed.). Prospect Heights, IL: Waveland Press.

Harari, O. (2002). *The leadership secrets of Colin Powell*. New York: McGraw-Hill.

Heifetz, R. (1994). *Leadership without easy answers*. Cambridge, MA: Harvard University Press.

Hillman, J. (1995). *Kinds of power*. New York: Doubleday/Currency.

Hughes, R. L., Ginnett, R. C., & Curphy, G. J. (2005). *Leadership* (5th ed.). New York: McGraw-Hill/Irwin.

Katz, D., & Kahn, R. (1978). *The social psychology of organizations*. New York: Wiley.

Komives, S. R., Lucas, N., & McMahon, T. R. (1998). *Exploring leadership: For college students who want to make a difference*. San Francisco: Jossey-Bass.

Kouzes, J., & Pozner, B. (2003). *The leadership challenge*. San Francisco: Jossey-Bass.

Linsky, M., & Heifetz, R. (2002). *Leadership on the line*. Boston: Harvard Business School Press.

Lipman-Blumen, J. (1996). *The connective edge: Leading in an interdependent world*. San Francisco: Jossey-Bass.

Manz, C., & Sims, H. (1989). *SuperLeadership*. Englewood Cliffs, NJ: Prentice Hall.

Mazlish, B. (1990). *The leader, the led, and the psyche*. Middletown, CT: Wesleyan University Press.

Napolitano, C. S., & Henderson, L. J. (1997). *The leadership odyssey: A self-development guide to new skills for new times*. San Francisco: Jossey-Bass.

Northouse, P. (2003). *Leadership: Theory and practice* (3rd ed.). Thousand Oaks, CA: Sage.

Osland, J. (1995). *The adventure of working abroad*. San Francisco: Jossey-Bass.

Pascale, R., Milleman, M., & Gioja, L. (2001). *Surfing the edge of chaos*. New York: Three Rivers Press.

Peters, T., & Waterman, R. H. (1988). *In search of excellence*. New York: Warner Books.

Phillips, D. (1992). *Lincoln on leadership*. New York: Warner Books.

Price, A. (2004). *Ready to lead?* San Francisco: Jossey-Bass.

Robinson, W. (2002). *Leading people from the middle: The universal mission of heart and mind*. Provo, UT: Executive Excellence Publishing.

Rost, J. (1993). *Leadership for the twenty-first century*. New York: Praeger.

Schein, E. H. (1997). *Organizational culture and leadership* (2nd ed.). San Francisco: Jossey-Bass.

Selznick, P. (1983). *Leadership in administration*. Berkeley: University of California.

Senge, P. M. (1990). *The fifth discipline: The art and practice of the learning organization*. New York: Doubleday-Currency.

Spears, L. (ed.). (1997). *Insights on leadership: Service, stewardship, spirit, and servant leadership*. New York: Wiley.

Stone, D. A. (2002). *Policy paradox: The art of political decision making* (Rev. ed.). New York: Norton.

Wheatley, M. J. (1999). *Leadership and the new science: Discovering order in a chaotic world* (2nd ed.). San Francisco: Berrett-Koehler.

Wilber, K. (2001). *A theory of everything*. Boston: Shambhala.

Wren, T. (1995). *The leader's companion*. New York: Free Press.

Yukl, G. (2005). *Leadership in organizations* (6th ed.). Englewood Cliffs, NJ: Prentice Hall.

Zaccaro, S. (2001). *The nature of executive leadership: A conceptual and empirical analysis of success*. Washington, DC: American Psychological Association.

3

Leadership Theory in Use

Leadership learning experiences will have the greatest substance and impact only when they take into account the existing research and the many available theories on leadership and its dynamics. Conference programs, listservs, benchmarking initiatives, and consultations provide ample evidence of the wide range of usable theories; for some of us, the availability of so many theories and models may seem overwhelming. An ongoing commitment to reading, sharing insights with colleagues, and applying theories to practice will help. This chapter offers a starting place by providing a brief summary of the historic evolution of leadership thought and by referring you to other sources that address the topic in greater detail. I will also provide introductions to a select few theories in current use and provide examples of how each might be adapted in programs to foster leadership learning.

Notions of Leadership

Numerous authors have summarized the changing notions of leadership over the years. Realizing that research, theory, and writing about leadership have changed over time is crucial to examining what might be relevant in any leadership learning initiative. The following summaries demonstrate that multiple theories are perpetually in use, with some stimulating more helpful and appropriate insight than others. Analyzing your own views and recognizing that your colleagues' perspectives may or may not differ from your own is also helpful as you engage with them.

A Simple Taxonomy

One of the most widely accepted taxonomies of leadership includes a progression from Great Man to trait to behavioral to situational and contingency to influence to reciprocal and finally to chaos and systems implications in leadership (Komives et al., 1998, 2007). A brief description of each follows.

Great Man

The Great Man notion of leading assumes that only certain individuals have the capacity to lead. These rare individuals are recognized for their superior ability and are noted as heroes and heroines for having an impact in their time that far outweighs the contributions of others. The adage "leaders are born, not made" is a product of this era. Leaders were thought to emerge from the circumstances of the day, and they rose to the top as a function of Darwinian survival-of-the-fittest dynamics. The Great Man notion is prevalent in art and literature through most of history up until the second half of the twentieth century. Today, models of heroic leading are still prevalent in popular media, such as film, television, and even computer-animated games. The dominance of the Great Man perspective is rooted in the presumptions of royalty and the privileged class traditions. When the industrial era of the early twentieth century spawned rags-to-riches anomalies such as Andrew Carnegie, these giants became the new heroes who were believed to have that special something that defined a leader.

Trait

Early twentieth century industrialization inspired fabled stories of men and women who rose to great power and privilege from immigrant and poor backgrounds. As they rose, these individuals competed with or substituted for former European aristocracy in the imagination of the public. They were still singled out as unique and special because of their ascent from obscurity to phenomenal wealth and power. The Great Man notion was still alive, but the focus shifted to identifying the particular traits found in leaders, instead of relying on family pedigree or opportunity to predict leadership ability. These new industrial-era leaders were distinguished by their imposing or attractive appearance, ingenuity, perseverance, and intelligence, and the sheer force of their interpersonal influence. Such traits were assumed to be natural characteristics rather than qualities developed through exposure, experience, or learning.

Behavioral

Eventually the Great Man and trait prediction perspectives expanded to include the burgeoning middle class that followed industrialization and the World Wars. The rise to leadership of men and women who previously had no preparation, privilege, or unique attributes needed to be explained somehow. Research and theorizing shifted to the behaviors of those who appeared successful at leading. The assumption that there was a best way to lead still dominated these behavioral studies. Some of the characteristics that seemed to be consistent among effective leaders included good communication skills, an ability to motivate others, service as a symbol or representative of followers, and the skill to balance the task and relational (maintenance) demands required to get the job done.

Situational and Contingency

Two observations challenged the behavioral analysis of leading. The first was that leaders did not display the same behaviors in all circumstances. The second was that different characteristics appeared to be more effective in some situations than others. These situational and contingency models attempted to determine which specific behaviors or characteristics would enhance a leader's effectiveness in a given environment. Sometimes the approach in situational models was to advise leaders to adapt their styles to fit the situation at hand. In other examples, situational and contingency models advocated that different kinds of leaders would be effective in different circumstances and that individuals should therefore be selected for leadership in the conditions that best matched their personal styles and strengths.

Influence

The situational and contingency models of leadership had considerable intuitive appeal. Because circumstances and who was most effective in responding to them varied, the situational and contingency models helped explain the dynamics that might occur as leaders attempted to lead. However, some situational variables seemed more constant than others. The ability to influence or create social change was consistently associated with qualities such as vision, charisma, credibility, and trust. These variables became part of the study of influence in relationships. And the study of relationships—rather than individuals who led—resulted in a shift to looking at leadership as a social exchange process. Power was recognized as an important part of analyzing influence and included different forms of power, such as directive and coercive as well as expert and referent. These different kinds of power were also found to affect the dynamics and sustainability of influence in leadership.

Reciprocal

The reciprocal view proposes that sustaining constructive relationships that result in the exchange of benefit should be one of the central features of effective leadership. If the core purpose or goal of leadership is to positively influence followers to participate, contribute, or give their best effort to a collective purpose, then it becomes much more important to focus on the mutually shaping experience of shared leadership. In the reciprocal view, leadership is a transaction that achieves something for all parties involved. Reciprocity does not necessarily suggest that everyone benefits equally; it simply recognizes that there is some form of exchange either in the moment or the future that minimally satisfies all participants.

Chaos or Systems

The addition of chaos theory and systems dynamics in the 2007 edition of *Exploring Leadership* demonstrates a recognition of the increasing complexity of life in the twenty-first century. Chaos theory recognizes that control and prediction of organizational functions are often impossible. However, even when chaos is assumed, recognition of broader systems interaction can provide new possibilities for understanding the world and leadership's role within it.

Bensimon, Neumann, and Birnbaum (1989) advocated a framework similar to that of Komives et al. (1998, 2007). The Bensimon et al. analysis replaced reciprocal models with two additional categories, cognitive and cultural.

Cognitive

Cognitive analysis of leadership examines how the way we think influences our perceptions of leaders and leadership behaviors. This recognizes that our notions of leadership are subjective and socially constructed. Regardless of what is intended through leadership, others may attribute purposes that were not at all anticipated by the leader. Cognitive analysis potentially exposes the embedded assumptions that are part of the perspectives summarized earlier. For example, if followers believe that leading is the purview of special individuals who have unusual capabilities, they are more likely to acquiesce to the authority of their perceived leaders. This would contribute to passivity in participants or group members and could undermine others' ability to contribute their full talent and capacity.

Cultural

Similar to cognitive analyses, the interpretation of leadership as a cultural phenomenon emphasizes that it is socially constructed and varies according to the particular culture. This view of leadership explores symbolic and representational roles in greater depth, and examines how leadership interactions foster shared meaning and expectations. Powerful methods such as stories and rituals create a shared sense of meaning, values, and beliefs in an organization or group, and can contribute to a stronger bond among leaders and participants.

The Komives et al. (1989, 2007) and Bensimon et al. (1989) taxonomies have great utility when we attempt to understand and explain the different views of leading and leadership that are endorsed by our colleagues, many of whom hold beliefs reflected in one or more of these perspectives. Only by explicitly acknowledging and discussing our differences and similarities do we have the opportunity to explore both the merits and limitations of each theory. An easy way to stimulate such a conversation is to ask a reflective question about the selection criteria for any given leadership learning opportunity. For example, one may ask, "Is there an application process, or are all students welcome and encouraged to participate? If credentials and applications are used, what lies underneath the questions? Is a list of previous accomplishments and titles requested? Are questions about motivation to learn and potential to benefit included?" Our processes implicitly, if not explicitly, communicate our views related to Great Man, trait, behavioral, situational and contingency, influence, reciprocal, cognitive, and cultural views of leadership.

Other Analyses of Leadership

Most leadership educators are finding it increasingly difficult to select from the many interesting and provocative theories and models of leadership. For more detailed information, Peter Northouse (2004) provides summary information about a broad number of leadership theories, and he also addresses how these theories can be used in practice. Likewise, Stephen Covey (2004) provides an analysis of leadership theories as an appendix to *The 8th Habit: From Effectiveness to Greatness*. Covey's analysis provides examples of authors and the dates their theories were published as well as focused summary statements that capture the essence of each theory.

In addition to Northouse and Covey's summaries, Kezar, Carducci, and Contreras-McGavin (2006) provide an analysis of various leadership theories categorized by philosophical context. This analysis is helpful because it challenges the reader to think critically about the purposes and mindsets on which leadership theories are based. Without understanding the philosophy beneath a theory, one might select a theory that does not align well with the particular campus environment or institutional mission. Kezar et al. identify four broad philosophical frames including positivist, social constructivist, critical, and postmodern. Even though it is difficult to categorize the many theories available to us using these frames, the analysis itself helps to bring attention to the inherent assumptions that might otherwise go unnoticed. This analysis also helps the reader relate historical and contemporary leadership ideas to how we view learning. For example, the philosophical assumptions of the cognitive and cultural leadership models complement shared learning perspectives more than Great Man or behavioral views. As we explored in Chapters One and Two, critical reflection about our assumptions of learning and leadership is essential if we are to create learning environments that foster, rather then thwart, leadership learning.

Select Leadership Models and Their Uses

The unfortunate reality in leadership learning is that identification of a leadership theory or theories is not always part of the explicit program design. This may be the result of the broad range of relevant theories now available. Or it may be the result of the fact that planning teams may have tried to agree to a common theory and abandoned the effort because it created so much conflict among the participants. Whatever the reason, examining what is espoused about leadership, even if it likely includes multiple perspectives, is important if we wish to create coherence in leadership learning.

Selecting a few leadership models to highlight is dangerous, as I am aware of many colleagues whose work has been substantial and has contributed much to the emerging understanding of leadership in today's world. But because it is not the purpose of this chapter or the broader book to be exhaustive in its summary of leadership studies and learning, I have chosen six models that are either relatively widely used or which I have found particularly useful in working with students. The models include Robert Greenleaf's servant leadership (1977; Greenleaf & Spears, 2002); James MacGregor Burns's transforming/transformational leadership (1978); James Kouzes and Barry Posner's Leadership Challenge (1987/2002); Joseph Rost's postindustrial leadership (1991); the Eisenhower grant ensemble's Social Change Model of Leadership Development (Higher Education Research Institute, 1994); and Susan Komives, Nance Lucas, and Tim McMahon's Relational Leadership (1998/2007).

Greenleaf's Servant Leadership

Overview

Having served most of his life in large, complex organizations—corporations, foundations, churches, and colleges and universities—Greenleaf developed his notion of leadership out of a concern that these organizations were not serving the world's needs. To a large extent, his concerns emerged from the turbulence of the 1960s and 1970s and the general sense of hopelessness and frustration expressed in student demonstrations and unrest. Because much of this discontent came in higher education settings, Greenleaf believed that colleges and universities had a special responsibility to address the underlying leadership issues that could begin to resolve the complex issues of the day. He asserted that whereas colleges directed considerable energy to preparing doctors, lawyers, ministers, teachers, engineers, and scholars, they devoted little attention to preparing graduates for leadership. He also pointed out that there was evidence that higher education actually discouraged rather than encouraged leadership involvement. Because Greenleaf's language references individuals rather than the process of shared leadership, it may appear that he advocated more of a positional view of leading.

However, he clearly communicated that educators needed to nurture the leadership potential that was latent in all young people.

Core Beliefs

Greenleaf asserted that leaders should be servants first because, as a result, those they serve would become "healthier, wiser, freer, more autonomous, more likely themselves to become servants" (1977, p.13). In Greenleaf's thinking, servant leadership requires individuals to possess several characteristics. Servant leaders

Must feel a sense of agency—that is, a willingness to act.

Must know what they want to accomplish, to have a dream in which to engage others.

Listen and seek to understand others, thus gaining strength and improving their ability to serve.

Communicate effectively and with imagination.

Establish priorities and pay the closest attention to the things that matter most.

Offer unconditional acceptance and empathy, although in some cases they expect more or better contributions from their followers.

Foresee the unforeseeable and have honed their intuition to recognize patterns that others do not see. Greenleaf asserts that this foresight is the central ethic of leadership. Ultimately, intuition and foresight allow servant leaders to be more aware and perceptive and grant them the confidence to face the unknown.

Implications and Use

Greenleaf's servant leadership ideas are older than most of the other leadership learning models in contemporary use. Those who espouse and use this model remain devoted to it and recommend a lifestyle informed by and reflective of its principles. Although servant leadership has many attributes reminiscent of heroic leading, Greenleaf clearly advocated that broader numbers of students were capable of and should be cultivated for leadership. Servant leadership is potentially a good fit for faith-based or other private institutions where there is a strong humanitarian emphasis. The characteristics of servant leadership could function as a framework for leadership development experiences, or they could be used to communicate the expectations of the community as it nurtures leadership in its members. The servant leadership perspective is broadly enough conceived that it could complement other more research-based and assessable models.

Burns's Transforming Leadership

Overview

Transforming leadership occurs when "one or more persons *engage* with others in such a way that leaders and followers raise one another to higher levels of motivation and morality" (1978, p. 20). This concept, revolutionary when it was first mentioned by John Downton (1973) and then gaining broader attention from Burns's advocacy, has stimulated more than four hundred doctoral dissertations in leadership studies since that time (Burns, 2003). Burns proposed that transforming leadership could be found in intellectual, revolutionary, opinion, group, legislative, and executive arenas. He distinguished transactional from transforming leadership and believed each had different attributes. Transactional leadership involved an exchange in which leaders set certain conditions for the performance of a function and then provided accompanying rewards to colleagues and followers who fulfilled the conditions. In transforming leadership, however, the focus was on recognizing and exploiting the needs or demands of potential followers. The transforming leader thereby looked for the motives of followers, sought to satisfy their higher needs, and engaged them fully in the process of achieving their goals and by doing so, linked leadership to collective purposes and actual social change. As Burns explained, through transforming leadership, "power bases are linked not as counterweights but as mutual support for common purpose" (1978, p. 20). When conceived in this way, transforming leadership has the potential to satisfy human needs and expectations as it transcends multiple demands and wants that would otherwise undermine effective leadership. Transforming leadership responds to higher levels of moral development through a commitment to reasoned and conscious values.

Bernard Bass (1985) extended Burns's transforming leadership and coined the popular term that has become synonymous with it: *transformational leadership*. Bass established the formal theory of transformational leadership as well as methods to measure the factors of leadership behavior attributed to it in the MultiFactor Leadership Questionnaire (Bass & Avolio, 1995).

Core Beliefs

Bass identified four components that are essential to putting transformational leadership into action. The first of these was inspirational motivation, which involved leaders' abilities to stimulate extraordinary performance in their followers, thus stirring them to see their potential in leadership. Idealized influence, the second component, was the ability to serve as a model for others by demonstrating trustworthiness and justifying the respect others had in their leaders. The third component, intellectual stimulation, was perceived as essential to innovation and change, and necessary to help leaders gain new insights and perspectives for understanding problems and questions. The final element of transformational leadership was individualized consideration, which reflected an investment on the part of transformational leadership, and drew out the best in followers by helping them develop to their fullest potential.

Implications and Use

Most students and scholars of leadership know of Burns's transforming leadership idea. The term *transformational leader* is used frequently; it sometimes explicitly refers to Burn's ideas, and other times it does not. The concept that leadership can transform followers and groups to a higher state of performance is inherently attractive. The distinction between transactional and transformational leadership is also a useful contrast because it is easy for leaders to want to think of themselves as transformational when, in fact, they are engineering transactions that are no more than trade-offs that meet individual or organizational needs. Both transactional and transformational approaches can play a role as we seek to encourage more effective leadership, but as Burns points out, each approach has unique merits. On a practical basis, the four components of transformational leadership could be used as a template for feedback from group members to help leaders gain greater insight into how participants perceive them. Because trust is so essential to many leadership interactions, the focus on trust that is central to idealized influence could be especially helpful. One of the greatest advantages of the transformational leadership model is that an instrument is available to measure it: the MultiFactor Leadership Questionnaire (MLQ). The MLQ is based on the Full Range Leadership Model (Bass & Avolio, 1994), which includes measures of transformational leadership, transactional leadership, nontransactional leadership, and outcomes of leadership. The MLQ and MLQT (MultiFactor Leadership Questionnaire for Teams) allow the individual and group to compile feedback that includes perspectives from all levels of the organization. This 360-degree feedback can serve as a powerful stimulus for understanding among all those involved.

Kouzes and Posner's Leadership Challenge

Overview

Kouzes and Posner wrote *The Leadership Challenge* (1987/2002) to push management to consider new possibilities of leadership. It was based on qualitative research with private and public sector middle and senior managers. The subjects in the initial study were asked to tell their "personal best" stories of leading; these data were compiled to establish a model and instrument to measure participants' responses. Kouzes and Posner sought to revitalize organizations of all types so that they could be more effective in the marketplace and in service to others. Although they based the model on managers who held positions of authority, they asserted that leadership was not the purview of a privileged few but rather needed to be cultivated more broadly at multiple levels. The Leadership Practices Inventory (Kouzes & Posner, 1988) evolved for use in assessing managers' and leaders' behavior related to the model. In addition, companion instruments to assess members' perspectives and a Student Leadership Practices Inventory-self for college students (Kouzes & Posner, 2005) are now available.

Core Beliefs

Kouzes and Posner found that leaders and members alike wanted leadership that exemplifies honesty, credibility, and vision as well as inspires trust and willingness in others. The *Student Leadership Planner* (2006) proposed that if leaders wanted to learn to be more effective, they needed to work with reflection, intention, and action. Moreover, they needed to incorporate five practices and ten commitments into their leadership behavior as a way to achieve greater success. The five practices and the accompanying commitments include:

1. Model the way
   - Finding your voice
   - Setting the example
2. Inspire a shared vision
   - Envisioning the future
   - Enlisting others
3. Challenge the process
   - Searching for opportunities
   - Experimenting and taking risks

4. Enable others to act
   - Fostering collaboration
   - Strengthening others
5. Encourage the heart
   - Recognizing contributions
   - Celebrating the values and victories

A helpful assortment of support materials has emerged to complement the Leadership Challenge model, but the five practices and ten commitments themselves are most useful because they are intuitively appealing and relatively easy to translate to leadership practice in a broad array of organizational contexts.

Implications and Use

Because the Leadership Challenge model is based on research conducted in a variety of settings, its use is widely applicable. The book is straightforward and can serve as a text for undergraduate students. The assessment instruments provide hands-on opportunities for leadership educators and students alike to compare their leadership inclinations to those of others. The *Student Leadership Planner* could be given to students as an ongoing guide or journal as they explore leadership questions independently. This text breaks down the leadership practices in greater detail and offers guidelines for how to enact the practice, and "stop and think" activities that drive the practice deeper. The guidelines could be used in either a curricular or cocurricular setting. Students involved in leadership roles on campus could be drawn together in a personal enrichment workshop or seminar with the *Planner* serving as an ongoing stimulus and organizer for discussion. The Leadership Challenge model may work best in more formal organizational settings, including student government, fraternal organizations, or academic clubs and honorary societies. Such organizations frequently rely on student leaders who can increase their effectiveness in leadership by learning methods of challenging, inspiring, enabling, and modeling that can improve organizational performance. For organizations that have more predictable structures, the idea of finding and encouraging the heart in members' engagement can significantly enhance motivation and participation of all.

Rost's Postindustrial Leadership

Overview

In most academic circles, Rost (1991/1993) has been recognized as the most influential voice to advocate that the leadership field turn from studying leading to developing leadership. His postindustrial definition portrayed leadership as "an influence relationship among leadership and their collaborators who intend real changes that reflect their mutual purposes" (1993, p. 99). He asserted that the concept of "leader" was irrelevant, primarily because so many of those in typically recognized leadership positions achieve little in terms of his definition for the new millennium. Although Rost acknowledged that there were still multiple forms of leadership, he proposed that the twenty-first century called for a new paradigm that would take into account the flattening of organizations as well as increased access to information enabled by advances in science, technology, and media.

Core Beliefs

Rost's "Leadership Development in the New Millennium" (1993) has been one of the most frequently cited justifications for what is increasingly becoming the norm for college and university leadership programs: a focus on leadership as a relational capacity that can be developed in anyone and that is dependent on mutual work. This is the first theory that moved so significantly away from seeing leadership capability as a singular trait of unique individuals and embraced the possibility that all people have leadership potential.

Implications and Use

Rost's views can be used to challenge those students and faculty who have become comfortable with conventional and positional ideas about leading. For students, reading the article or book can help them begin to deconstruct assumptions about what may not be appropriate or useful in many of the experiences they will face in college and afterward. Short and to the point, "Leadership Development in the New Millennium" offers a number of meaty ideas to stimulate long and interesting discussions. Rost offers five points that could function as the framework for a discussion about new millennium leadership and thus involve students in shaping their own leadership experience. These five points include to stop concentrating on the leader, to conceive of leadership as an episodic affair, to train people to use influence, to develop people's ability to work within noncoercive relationships, and to help people understand the nature of real—that is, transformative—change (pp. 102–107). Because both Rost and Burns focus on transformation, their texts can easily be used to illustrate complementary perspectives.

The "Ensemble's" Social Change Model of Leadership Development

Overview

It may seem odd to see the term "ensemble" in relation to a leadership model. The word was chosen collectively by the individuals who created the Social Change Model of Leadership Development in order to convey the nature of the creation process as well as the core of the model. The ensemble sought to focus attention on the process of leadership while promoting the values of equity, social justice, self-knowledge, personal empowerment, collaboration, citizenship, and service. This model provided a framework for use in preparing college students for leadership that was not dependent on position and authority to stimulate change.

Core Beliefs

The Social Change Model of Leadership Development focused on student learning and development to increase self-knowledge, enhance leadership competence, and result in positive social change on campus or in the community beyond. The model is based on seven core values popularly referred to as the 7 C's (Higher Education Research Institute, 1996). These seven values are sorted into three levels that are deemed important to social change leadership:

1. Individual
   - Consciousness of self
   - Congruence
   - Commitment
2. Group
   - Collaboration
   - Common purpose
   - Controversy with civility
3. Society and community
   - Citizenship

The creators of the Social Change model believed that the individual, group, and societal and community spheres interacted with each other in a dynamic and creative way to achieve the ultimate goal of social change.

The Social Change model proposed an experientially based leadership development process that included attention to the physical setting, task definition, recruitment of participants, research and redefinition, division of responsibility, group process and feedback, and creation of sustainable outcomes. Through this group life cycle, groups can build leadership capacity as a natural part of their experiences. Another important dimension to the

Social Change model was that leadership educators would begin to see themselves as part of the process of leadership development, empowering students to be more invested in and responsible for their own experiences. Students and leadership educators would then join together in the shared journey of leadership learning.

Implications and Use

The Social Change Model of Leadership Development emphasizes the importance of students exploring their personal development journey as part of leadership learning. The individual variables of consciousness of self, congruence, and commitment serve as an excellent stimulus to questions such as, "Who am I and what do I stand for?" Addressing the problems of bad leadership that I will discuss in greater detail in Chapter Five cannot be undertaken without nudging students into the journey of personal understanding. The group variables of collaboration, common purpose, and controversy with civility introduce dynamics that frequently go unnoticed when leadership is exerted in a group. This emphasis on collaborating toward a common purpose and recognizing disagreement and constructive criticism as assets rather than impediments can revolutionize group process.

Another important aspect of the Social Change model is that it poses citizenship as the outcome of leadership. Citizenship can be enacted in a variety of contexts—a living group, community, business, politics, or service. By conceiving citizenship broadly, students will more readily recognize different forms of democratic engagement that incorporate the preservation of individual rights as well as responsibilities. The Social Change Model of Leadership Development may be particularly effective in working with students who are committed to philanthropy, community service, and service-learning. At the heart of much of student volunteerism is a desire to improve the lives of those served, to protect the environment, or to help those in need of educational or social enrichment. The Social Change model could demonstrate to students that their commitment to serving others might also need to include working with their peers and those being served to rectify the conditions that create the need for service. Might that actually be a more deeply informed and potentially more influential form of citizenship?

Developing Non-Hierarchical Leadership on Campus (Outcalt, Faris, & McMahon, 2001) provides a variety of examples of how the Social Change model can be applied to practice. Some of the examples demonstrate the important shift to shared leadership that I noted earlier. Other examples illustrate the importance of establishing a culture of leadership that builds capacity among a broad number of faculty, staff, and students in a campus community.

Further implications and uses of the Social Change Model of Leadership Development are noted in Chapter Five. In addition, work is under way to create assessment instruments for use with the Social Change model. Initial work by Tracy Tyree (1998) was used as the basis for a number of items on the Multi-Institution Study of Leadership (Komives & Dugan, 2006). This study involved fifty-two campuses in a cross-institutional study to measure various aspects of their leadership initiatives. More specifically, it was designed to measure the degree to which the seven factors of the Social Change model were part of the campus culture. Interpretation of this data is under way and will have great influence on how educators approach comprehensive leadership in the future.

Komives, Lucas, and McMahon's Relational Leadership

Overview

The title *Exploring Leadership: For College Students Who Want to Make a Difference* (Komives et al., 1998, 2007) describes precisely how the Relational Leadership model differs from the others summarized in this chapter. The authors aimed to affirm that all members of a group or organization, regardless of their title or role, can be a part of the leadership process. This text set forth the definition of leadership as a "relational and ethical process of people together attempting to accomplish positive change" (2007, p. ix), an interpretation that combined aspects of Rost's definition (1991/1993) as well as the change and common good elements of the Social Change model (Higher Education Research Institute, 1994). The relational model of leadership addressed college students through their experiences and in language that they could easily understand.

Core Beliefs

The authors portray Relational Leadership as a model, rather than a theory. The model comprises five primary components: inclusive, empowering, purposeful, ethical, and process-oriented. The inclusive component states that in order to tap the talent of all potential contributors, leadership needs to focus on creating an organizational culture that communicates the worth of all people. The empowering component is based on establishing a climate of trust and respect. The authors recognize power as a natural part of most settings but assert that all members should be encouraged to recognize their full right and opportunity to participate. The purposeful component refers to the importance of drawing all members together with a commitment to work toward a common vision. The ethical and moral component introduces the central importance of values and standards in good leadership. The final component, process-oriented, draws attention to the formation, decision-making, and action of groups as they seek to achieve their goals.

The Relational Leadership model requires a depth of self-knowledge that is achieved through personal reflection and introspection as well as a growing awareness of group processes. *Exploring Leadership* includes summary concepts and additional readings at the end of every chapter for those students who want to learn more. More important, the text provides activities that can be used to put the components of the Relationship Leadership model into practice.

Implications and Use

Relational Leadership could be used in either a curricular or cocurricular setting. It is straightforward enough that noncredit seminars or reading groups could work progressively through the book with ease. An instructor's guide is available as a download-able file, which helps a great deal in planning courses or seminars. In addition to providing guidance for relationally oriented lead-ership through the five components of the model, the authors define in simple ways what a healthy organization would look like. Relational Leadership moves the focus away from positional leaders and onto creating healthy organizations, thus emphasizing the shared responsibility of all members to create better organiza-tions, a major benefit of this model. Part four of *Exploring Leader-ship* summarizes theories and models of change that are extremely helpful for students as they seek to make a difference; the Social Change model is incorporated into this section. Part five also includes new material about leadership identity and helpful ideas about renewing self, groups, and organizations. Considering the highly pressured lives of many undergraduates in today's colleges and universities, the advice offered in the last section could be used to help students achieve greater balance, purpose, and effec-tiveness in their lives.

What Does All This Mean?

Exploring the ways we have viewed leadership over time and getting up to speed on contemporary models are important steps on the journey toward understanding leadership. Using these mod-els literally and as if they were infallible destines us only to frus-tration. As Bensimon, Neumann, and Birnbaum (1989) indicate, "as long as leaders look to researchers to identify specific activities that will enable them to be more effective, they are doomed to disappointment. Research can provide only trivial and superficial responses to those who seek specific answers" (p. 69).

New students of leadership are often seduced into simplistic notions of leadership because, as Kezar et al. (2006) note, "In our experience teaching leadership, the traditional, functionalist behavior or power and influence strategies, for example, are easier for practitioners to understand initially as they are part of our popular culture and take less analytic work to tackle" (p. 157). If we naively accept leadership theory and models, we risk misusing otherwise helpful ideas in inappropriate circumstances or, perhaps more dangerously, using ill-informed or poorly conceptualized models in situations where effective models are desperately needed.

We are in this together—leadership educators, those who aspire to and accept the call to leadership, and all those who hope to reap the benefit of improved leadership in our communities, nation, and around the globe. *The National Leadership Index 2005: A National Study of Confidence in Leadership* (Quinley, 2005) underscored both the challenges and the opportunities that citizens of the United States believe they face. The bad news of this study was that there is broad and generalized concern about the condition of leadership in the United States, a level of concern that calls for something different from what we typically conceive of or observe in leadership. The good news was that average citizens, workers, and community members see themselves as part of the leadership problem because they lack critical information about issues that are important to the public welfare. Citizens of the United States also expressed optimism about the future leadership of the country, especially if more women became involved in leadership.

4

Preparing Leadership for the Future

Chapter Three framed how we have come to know and understand leadership. It also summarized six theories of leadership that are used widely in college and university leadership programs. As background and preparation for Chapter Five, this chapter introduces research related to the workplace of the future and offers models and theories that educators can use to prepare students for the leadership skills they need in the twenty-first century.

Similar to the disclaimer offered in Chapter Three, this chapter does not attempt to cover all the ideas and models that could be helpful; there are simply too many good ideas that are emerging to attempt such a lofty goal. I include the models and theories that have the best basis in research and that address leadership learning in the very practical context of work. I begin the chapter by introducing the analysis by Frederick T. Evers, James C. Rush, and Iris Berdrow (1998) of the workplace of the future and higher education's efforts to prepare students; in particular, I focus on their findings that the leadership skills on which students need to improve the most include managing people and tasks and mobilizing innovation and change. I then discuss ways to enhance training and development in these two skill areas. I present the concepts of emotional intelligence (Goleman, Boyatzis, & McKee, 2002) and connective leadership (Lipman-Blumen, 1996) as ways to enhance students' abilities to manage people and tasks. To address skills related to mobilizing innovation and change, I draw on Moss-Kanter's discussion of the life cycles of organizations (2004) and Hagberg's (description of the inner journey of leadership

(2003). Finally, I conclude the chapter by raising two questions that will prepare the way for the model I will introduce in Chapter Five. I will address the first question of how college students come to see their own potential in leadership through the leadership identity development research by Susan Komives et al. (2006). Addressing the second question of how students discover the leadership questions most needing their attention, I will use the adaptive leadership concept of Ronald Heifetz (1994) and Heifetz and Marty Linsky (2002).

The Bases of Competence

One of the classic questions for educators is how students' experiences during the collegiate years prepare them for the workplace. Whether educators like it or not, the increased commoditization of a college degree has created greater public expectation that a college education should result in career success.

The issue of employability and effectiveness at work has become all the more complex as a result of the changes taking place in the workplace. The drumbeat of globalization, the relentless pace of technology, the flattening of organizational structures, and greater reliance on teams are just some of the changes that new graduates face. If they are not ready for the workplace of the future, graduates may not find the advancement opportunities or career satisfaction they seek.

Through the Making the Match project, Evers and his colleagues sought to determine the degree of fit between the skills possessed by college graduates and the qualities that employers sought in their employees. Although Evers et al. conducted their study with a sample of Canadian students and employers, at least one study with U.S. students and employers found similar results. A study of employers of Miami University graduates (Business Development Directives and Garrett Consulting, 2005) confirmed many of the trends that were identified in the Making the Match project. In the following sections, I urge readers to pay particular attention to the extent to which the findings of Evers et al. may apply to their own unique contexts.

The Making the Match research found that there were four broad skill areas that employers valued most. These included managing self, communicating, managing people and tasks, and mobilizing innovation and change. Each of these four areas was composed of more detailed items. For example, the items under the managing self skill area were learning, personal organization and time management, personal strengths, and problem solving skills. The communicating cluster included working well with others, listening, and oral and written communication skills. Coordinating, decision making, leadership and influence, managing conflict, and planning and organizing composed the managing people and tasks cluster. Finally, ability to conceptualize, creativity, risk taking, and visioning constituted the mobilizing innovation and change cluster. For the Making the Match study, graduates rated themselves and their employers also rated them on each of the skill areas.

Graduates rated themselves highest in managing self and communicating and lowest in managing people and tasks and mobilizing innovation and change. Employers of recent graduates perceived the same pattern. The main problem, however, was that the areas in which employers wanted the greatest skill were just the opposite; employers wanted workers who scored higher in managing people and tasks and mobilizing innovation and change. The project further determined that this mismatch could not be corrected by teaching interventions alone. Instead, more complex experiences such as encouraging students to determine a vision for their future or taking risks in creative problem solving were more likely to help students learn how to mobilize innovation and change. The bottom line was that in order to help students learn the skills that match the needs of their employers, collegiate institutions need to broaden their definition of learning and tackle the more complex, and more lasting, skill areas of managing people and tasks and mobilizing innovation and change.

The Making the Match project serves as a useful conversation starter for leadership learning because it identifies the four broad skill areas employers value and indicates the degree to which students succeed in each skill area. Experiences inside and outside the classroom help college graduates enter the workplace with better self-management and communication skills. However, in the areas of managing people and tasks and mobilizing innovation and change, a gap exists; students enter the workplace at a lower ability level than employers expect them to be and the future will require. These two gap areas just happen to be areas in which focused and purposeful leadership learning might be able to offer the greatest potential for improvement and thus add the greatest value for our institutions and graduates.

A follow-up study (Evers, Power, & Mitchell, 2003) using roundtables, interviews, and meetings determined that communication, project management, creativity, and leadership form a pyramid of advanced level skills that are essential for the future success of Canadian organizations and businesses. Creativity and leadership appear at the top of the advanced skills list, confirming the validity of the original Making the Match study.

The Making the Match study and the Bases of Competence model provide evidence of the strengths and challenges that Canada, and likely other countries, face in preparing college graduates for the workplace of the future. Leadership educators can use such a mandate to build the case for the importance of leadership learning and to cultivate relationships throughout the campus community and beyond that would provide opportunity for students to develop greater creativity and leadership. Ultimately, the Bases of Competence model could help students understand the importance of what they are learning about leadership. Students' competencies would need to be developed over time through multiple and progressive experiences. Sticking with a commitment and a purposeful plan would help students acquire the insights, skills, and competencies necessary to become valuable, contributing members of work teams and communities that need their full talents.

The following sections describe additional models that provide greater detail and substance for the competency development areas of managing people and tasks and mobilizing innovation and change.

Managing People and Tasks

The Making the Match study identified five essential subelements in the managing people and tasks area. Of these five, three had developing and managing relationships as the core, and the other two had a partial relational focus. Before turning to the other research and theory that relates to the Making the Match findings, I will describe the five managing people and tasks elements to further detail the competencies that should be addressed in leadership learning.

The first subelement, coordinating, included working with peers and subordinates and encouraging positive and productive group relationships. The second, decision making, involved making informed decisions based on a variety of evidence and weighing the political and ethical dimensions of the decision. Although some decision making could be done in isolation, identifying and considering the points of view of those being affected had important relational implications. The third, leadership and influence, focused on motivating, providing direction, and guiding the contributions of peers and subordinates. The fourth, managing conflict, involved seeing the sources of conflict at all levels of the organization and taking steps to overcome the disharmony that caused the discord. The fifth, planning and organizing, included being able to determine the actions needed to complete a project or initiative as well as delegating, monitoring, and revising the plan as teams worked together to accomplish their tasks.

The majority of the descriptors for the managing people and tasks elements are in the interpersonal relations domain. With such a strong relational focus, it is clear that one of the primary leadership challenges is reading and appropriately responding to interpersonal clues. This is essentially the area of emotional intelligence.

Emotional Intelligence

Analysis by Goleman, Boyatzis, and McKee (2002) of the relevance of emotional intelligence to leadership yielded startling results. Whereas many previous studies of leadership had proposed that intellectual capacity was most central to leadership, the research by Goleman et al. asserted that emotional intelligence was primal, meaning that it was both the first and most important aspect of leadership. In fact, they found that 50 to 70 percent of employees' perceptions of their environment were related to the climate established by leadership, and every 1 percent improvement in the service climate correlated with a 2 percent improvement in revenue in for-profit settings.

Goleman et al. also found that the influence of emotional conditions in an organization were related to the way in which the limbic system—the center that controls emotions and feelings—operates in humans. The limbic system is an open loop system, meaning that it incorporates and interprets stimuli outside itself. As it interprets the behaviors of others or of the broader organization, an individual's limbic system changes. Thus the moods of a colleague or of someone in leadership affect not only individuals' sense of what is happening but actually change their physiology and therefore their emotions. This emotional contagion influences offices, organizations, and teams for good or ill.

That leadership climate influences profitability as well as individuals' attitudes and behaviors provides compelling evidence that emotional intelligence should receive greater focus in leadership learning.

Core Findings

Based on the powerful influence or contagion of emotions in an organization, Goleman et al. identified several leadership competencies that deserve special attention. These include four broad areas with subparts in each. The first area, self-awareness, includes emotional self-awareness, accurate self-assessment, and self-confidence. The second, self-management, includes self-control, transparency, adaptability, achievement, initiative, and optimism. The third area, social awareness, consists of empathy, organizational awareness, and service. The fourth area, relationship management, comprises inspiration, influence, development of others, change catalyst, conflict management, and teamwork and collaboration. Collectively, these four broad areas—self-awareness, self-management, social awareness, and relationship management—provide an umbrella under which the subparts fall and provide support. Leadership learning that addresses and focuses on these four areas is more purposeful and effective in creating an emotional climate that results in group goal attainment.

Focusing on the four areas can be very difficult for some of those who need to enhance them most. The analysis by Goleman et al. on emotional intelligence in leadership found that those who achieve leadership in hierarchical settings are vulnerable to a particularly negative dynamic they described as the CEO disease. This disease resulted from a lack of feedback given to those in managerial leadership as they climbed in the organizational hierarchy. Those at the top had the least access to honest and helpful feedback, and were the most likely to misread the climate that they fostered in their organizations. Further, those who were the poorest performers had the most unrealistic estimate of their own capabilities. This combination of little feedback at high levels and the unrealistic self-assessments of poor performers is a recipe for disaster in organizations that need to tap the talent of all their members.

Implications and Use

Goleman et al. indicate that a significant portion of leadership learning occurs from adolescence through the early twenties. During this period of youth, the brain's capacity is still developing. If educators pay attention to developing emotional intelligence, they can set up patterns of functioning that will pay off handsomely in attributes such as drive to achieve, collaboration, and persuasion—capacities that can be important in tackling many leadership challenges.

Learning to be more emotionally aware and skilled is not a matter of learning how to manipulate others into seeing oneself in a certain way. Rather, becoming emotionally intelligent is the result of being more reflective, seeking and incorporating input from a variety of individuals and sources, and being flexible enough to adjust to the needs of participants. Realism, optimism, and authenticity are the characteristics that distinguish true emotional intelligence from the game face that some put on to feign emotional intelligence and responsiveness.

Goleman et al. recommend five key questions that individuals seeking to enhance their emotional intelligence should consider. The key questions are (1) Who do I want to be? (2) Who am I now? (3) How do I get from here to there? (4) How do I make change stick? and (5) Who can help me? These straightforward questions could be used in a workshop or teaching environment to help students progress through the process of self-discovery that will lead to greater emotional intelligence. Another strategy could be to incorporate these questions into the ongoing discipline of a living group or student organization. By periodically taking the time to reflect on these questions, exchanging perspectives candidly with each other, and challenging each other to work for improvement, a group of students can exponentially improve the climate and connection within their community.

One of the most interesting and perhaps most important points made by Goleman et al. is that learning to cultivate emotional intelligence results in the ability to access and trust our intuition, a point that Malcolm Gladwell (2005) reinforces in his popular book *Blink*. Robert Nash defines intuition as the "nonconscious rational mind" that gives us "an immediate sense of the 'right' thing to do when we let the solution to a dilemma just come to our minds" (2002, p. 68). Intuition is a guide to leadership actions when it provides a glimpse of the best strategy or the right way to work with others. Intuition is helpful as a guide for our own actions and it is equally important when we face the decision of whether to accord trust to others who seek to exercise leadership over us.

How many times has history proved that individuals, sometimes in the tens of thousands, denied their intuition about demonic or abusive leaders and did nothing to resist them? In some ways, dictatorial and autocratic leaders fulfill a human need to be cared for and directed. Because of this need, we can sometimes tolerate abusive behaviors when we observe mistreatment of others. Books by Jean Lipman-Blumen (2004) and Barbara Kellerman (2004) on bad leaders provide much more detail and concrete examples on how this occurs. What can be drawn from Goleman et al., Gladwell, Lipman-Blumen, and Kellerman is that one of the important shared responsibilities among leaders and members is to understand and protect against the potential of bad leadership. Greater emotional intelligence would likely help members and citizens more keenly discern the trustworthiness of their leaders.

To acquire greater emotional intelligence, we must trust our intuition. Especially in academic communities where rational, scientific, and presumably objective fact dominates, honoring the importance of intuition is particularly challenging. In such settings, many of us discount emotionally informed insights because the prevailing culture validates cognition rather than intuition—that is, knowing versus feeling. Research on women's ways of leading (Helgeson, 1990, 1995) indicated that one of the greatest strengths that women potentially bring to leadership is more intuitional insight, which seems to validate the importance of intuition and emotional intelligence.

Developing deeper emotional intelligence is critical to learning how to be more effective in leadership and becoming more discerning followers. The bad leaders about whom Kellerman and Lipman-Blumen warn us can be discerned if we trust our intuition and emotional intelligence more fully. Only through developing this capacity can we begin to trust the communities and organizations in which we live and work.

Emotional intelligence is a capacity that helps leaders develop more authentic relations with others and thus informs the philosophy known as connective leadership.

Connective Leadership

Lipman-Blumen (1996) addressed the importance of the relational aspects of leadership when she proposed the concept of connective leadership, which combines a number of styles and does not rely on any specific, prescriptive role. Lipman-Blumen found that connective leadership arose when those exercising leadership moved from stage two to stage three in her model. This shift occurred when the leadership paradigm changed "from independence to interdependence, from control to connection, from competition to collaboration, from individual to group, and from tightly linked geopolitical alliances to loosely coupled global networks" (p. 226). Stage three was also more focused on the group than on the individual. Connective leaders became catalysts by using any one of the nine styles available to them rather than using one or two styles in a more parochial way. The nine styles were grouped into three broader categories: direct, instrumental, and relational. The direct style focused on mastering tasks through intrinsic, competitive, and power strategies. The instrumental style relied on personal, social, and entrusting strategies to maximize interactions. The relational style included collaborative, contributory, and vicarious means to contribute to others' task accomplishments. Rather than focusing on control or independent decision making that drew attention to themselves, connective leaders used a variety of ethical and instrumental actions to tackle complex situations. Connective leaders were effective because they brokered and matched the needs and interests of diverse individuals and groups and sparked confidence and creativity in followers. Finally, because they were committed to group rather than individual accomplishment, connective leaders served as mentors to others and celebrated the accomplishments of everyone from colleagues to strangers.

Core Findings

Connective leadership is clearly not a genetic attribute nor is it an archetype. In fact, Lipman-Blumen suggested that the connective leaders in her study learned to use a variety of styles because they were forced to explore alternatives when other more narrow styles of leading failed them. By necessity, then, connective leaders test and modify their approaches to respond to the different conditions they confront on a daily basis. By sharing credit with others, connective leaders draw together disparate individuals and groups to focus on common objectives. Influence under these circumstances becomes a two-way and perhaps even a multi-directional proposition as constituencies align to strive for broader goals while achieving their individual but interdependent objectives.

Lipman-Blumen proposed that the assumptions of interdependence and reciprocity drew others to the connective leader. Long-term cooperation that creates a sense of obligation to repay or return good faith and good will is the connective leader's goal. When individuals feel that their futures are mutually linked, they are eager to reach out and assure one another's success. This establishes a set of conditions on which many ongoing relationships can build: trust, sponsorship, encouragement, and visible and invisible collaboration.

A growing sense of authentic and accountable leadership is one of the most powerful outcomes of connective leadership. Even though authenticity is difficult to define and consequently difficult to cultivate, it plays a key role when colleagues and followers are considering whether to invest themselves in a relationship with a leader. Individuals choose to fully participate in relationships with connective leaders because such leaders are committed beyond their own egoistic needs and benefits. As Lipman-Blumen explains in *The Connective Edge*, "It appears that when leaders fully commit themselves to the cause and demand the same from supporters, their authenticity magnetizes supporters and ignites their dedication" (1996, p. 245).

Implications and Use

Connecting and collaborating do not come naturally in collegiate settings. The scientific positivism of the academic environment focuses largely on individual and competitive action. However, Lipman-Blumen makes the point that the world of the future requires more collective and consonant action. Her connective leadership model could serve as an alternative paradigm to the traditional model of academic achievement in which scholars isolate themselves in their studies and struggle with ideas on their own. Indeed, many academic programs are beginning to use team projects and group work more frequently at all levels of collegiate learning. First-year student seminars can introduce new students to engaged learning opportunities through service-learning or through preparation and delivery of team projects. Facilitators can encourage students to deconstruct these early experiences of working with groups by asking them to critically examine how effective groups work and why. Only by teasing out such lessons can students learn the importance and power of group learning for subsequent team projects. As students rise to advanced-level courses, projects and teams become even more important. When they encounter groups in senior capstone projects, students should be able to conceptualize effective teamwork and engage with each other to enhance the quality of their work—in contrast to what sometimes is more of a divide-and-conquer mentality.

One of the difficult challenges Lipman-Blumen raised is the way the public media continues to reinforce, and thereby perpetuate, stage two leadership—the kind that relies on static approaches and does not embrace the connective and collaborative approaches that are more likely to be effective in some of today's and most assuredly tomorrow's organizations. It is easy to find this same kind of resistance to stage three connective leadership in campus media. If campus leadership learning advocates connective leadership while the student newspaper calls for decisive, dramatic, and solo leadership, the tension between the two is likely to become frustrating for all involved. Student government advisers could help the campus community reconcile such competing notions of leadership by holding at least an annual meeting among newspaper reporters and student leaders to discuss their differences. This kind of meeting would help expand the conceptual frames of both leaders and reporters so that the true and necessary complexity of leading in student government would be recognized. Ultimately, a broader group of students would learn the challenges of political leadership and would begin to see how to help shape, respond to, and engage in grassroots participation.

In essence, emotional intelligence and connective leadership can enhance the detail and depth of leadership learning among students. These concepts help by providing specific insights on how students and graduates can become more effective in managing people and tasks, an area where employers seek improved performance and where colleges and universities are perceived to be less effective than employers would like.

Mobilizing Innovation and Change

The other broad area where the Making the Match research found a gap was in preparing college graduates to mobilize innovation and change. This could very well be the most important area in which higher education and leadership learning can have an impact in the twenty-first century. Creating environments that can adjust to changing global economic markets will be essential for those countries where manufacturing and production are moving to less expensive production environments—leaving innovation, product development, and research to countries with high levels of education and high expectations, standards, and costs of living. The challenge is to create new employment opportunities above and instead of the workplaces and products to which we have become accustomed.

Leadership that fosters a willingness to change is central to the evolving dynamics of all types of organizations: for-profit, not-for-profit, governmental, education, the arts, and others. Willingness to change stems from participants' trust in leadership and confidence in the organization's ability to make the changes that are deemed necessary. To understand this change-oriented climate, we turn to the work of Rosabeth Moss-Kanter.

Confidence

The title of Moss-Kanter's book, *Confidence: How Winning Streaks and Losing Streaks Begin and End* (2004), says it all. By presenting the results of studies in for-profit and social entrepreneurship settings, political groups, and sports teams, she explains how organizations can restore confidence that high goals are achievable. Any organization can be swept into success by good economic conditions or accidents of time and place. However, most organizations find themselves in environments where their future is determined more by the spirit of the organization than anything else. Thus Moss-Kanter addressed the question of what allows an organization to maintain a winning streak or get back on track to turn around a losing streak. She proposed that it can be summed up in the central idea of restoring confidence.

"Confidence is the bridge connecting expectations and performance, investment and results" (Moss-Kanter, 2004, p. 3). When an organization is improving, it has confidence in new possibilities and keeps moving forward. When an organization is declining, it must restore confidence in order to turn the tide of downward momentum. What Moss-Kanter discovered was that there were fairly predictable indicators of decline, and, more important, there were concrete and actionable strategies that could be used to reverse an organization's losing streak. Striving to create winning streaks and learning how leadership restores confidence could significantly improve the contribution of any worker, new or experienced.

Core Findings

In Moss-Kanter's analyses, deteriorating organizational health involved a combination of variables. Some of these caused the decline; others were a response to it. First, communication decreased. Participants disconnected from each other by avoiding meetings, turning inward, and refusing to talk to one another. They dodged unpleasant conversations about issues that most, if not all, members recognized as problematic. Once this losing streak began, criticism and blame increased; colleagues and members scapegoated and attacked each other. Once former colleagues began targeting each other, self-doubt overcame still more people, and widespread anxiety took hold. This cloud of criticism caused a reduced level of respect for one another, further reinforcing a sense of mediocrity. Isolation and reclusive behaviors became the norm, resulting in low social interaction outside only the essential organizational context. Reclusive behavior engendered self-absorption, low trust, and a focus on individual welfare, regardless of the cost to others. One of the greatest penalties of this individualistic self-preservation was that rifts widened and inequities grew. The trust level was so fractured that others were shut out of decision making, creating cliques and unhealthy competition for favors and advantage. Negativity hung over the organization and pervaded most of the interactions between members. Energy declined, burnout became epidemic, ambition diminished, and a loser mind-set characterized nearly every action and interaction. Learned helplessness locked participants in a crippling tailspin in which they accepted losing as inevitable. Ironically, trying to minimize loss often became the aspiration in these settings. Finally, the negativity was so overwhelming that striving for anything better seemed nearly impossible. Indeed, the climate of a losing organization became one of hopelessness, and those who experienced such a climate struggled to find ways to restore hope. Moss-Kanter notes, "When accountability, collaboration, and initiative are replaced by a culture of anger and blame, fragmentation and conflict, vicious cycles are set into motion" (2004, p. 140).

Winning streaks, though, were dramatically different. Moss-Kanter's research determined that effective organizations exhibited four types of confidence: in oneself, one another, the system, and external support. Self-confidence was characterized by high expectations shared by all organization members. Positive, supportive, and team-oriented behaviors established confidence in one another. Organizational structures and routines reinforced that confidence in the system was justified. When these three types of confidence were present, the fourth type followed: confidence that external networks would support them and would provide the necessary resources for the organization to be successful. The challenge for organizations on a losing streak was how to instill confidence in these four areas.

Establishing an atmosphere that conveyed belief in people and their power to make a difference was essential to turning an organization's losing streak around, because it helped organization members begin to realize that their time and effort mattered. During the turnaround process, entrenched hopelessness and negativity lingered, but leadership was able to redirect this negative energy by challenging members to pursue nobler and bigger causes to which they could contribute. The causes might include anything from designing and producing a new product to improving the quality of performance or surviving intense competition with a rival. When positivity began to emerge, leaders worked diligently to reawaken initiative and enterprise. During this initial phase, nurturing, funding, and providing support were essential. The best way to help members feel the momentum of change was through sponsorship of small wins that would immediately demonstrate that conditions could change and that renewed success was achievable.

Rebuilding an organization and setting it on a winning path depended on establishing systems of accountability, collaboration, and initiative. Individual and system accountability required a willingness to foster the straight talk through which members could address real concerns, communicate clear expectations, and make information readily accessible and transparent. Mutual respect, communication, and collaboration required initiating and structuring conversations in ways that reinforced respect and inclusion of all participants, identified shared goals and mutually agreed-on definitions of success. Initiative, imagination, and innovation required opening opportunities to pursue new ideas, treating members as competent in contributing their expertise in their work, and encouraging the initial small wins and innovations from the ground up.

Implications and Use

The variables that define losing and winning streaks have great intuitive appeal. I have used this model in numerous presentations to student groups and organizations. The result each time has been immediate recognition of the work that needed to be tackled. Student government and fraternal organizations are two specific types of groups that tend to see the dynamics of losing and winning streaks most readily, but other organizations may see the merit as well. Educators can easily adapt the confidence model to a workshop session where they lay out the framework, give students a chance to individually reflect and assess their own perceptions, and then invite students to share and compare their thoughts in a larger group. Such a strategy can begin to open the communication and give permission to students to deal with the real issues that their organizations face. Because student governments and fraternal organizations turn over their formal leadership on at least an annual basis, the confidence model can be particularly effective as a stimulus for reflecting on the organization's past and future.

Student organization advisers of all sorts look for ways to understand the dynamics of their organizations and how to craft a useful role for themselves. Knowing how to assess the health of an organization by using the confidence model, advisers could begin to help student organization members better analyze the ebb and flow of organization life and stay aware of the trends they observe. If there is a downturn in communication and organization participation, it is best to address the change, rather than make excuses of pressing calendars and competing demands. The downturn should be considered an indication of declining commitment that may foretell a losing streak. The organization adviser would then be able to intervene, talk about the real issues, and then help the organization members restore the winning streak. The role of the student organization adviser could be transformed into one of teaching what healthy organizations look like and how winning ways can consistently become part of more campus and community organizations.

The confidence model is also a useful lens to assess an organization's or group's readiness for change. Learning this tool and others will help teach that leadership is a powerful way to sustain positive organizations that meet human needs. The next area we explore is how to help students discover core purposes for the leadership they hope to learn and demonstrate.

Soul Leadership

One of my fascinations with leadership has been its origins in the guts, hearts, or souls of those who choose to lead. This fascination has led me to ask many individuals and panels to describe what they believe to be the most important variables in leadership. I often raise this question during the guest leader panel of the LeaderShape Institute when we host it on our campus. The panel takes place on the evening of the third day of this six-day

intensive, personal journey toward discovering vision and learning to lead with integrity. It never fails that at least one of the
panelists, and usually more, will say that the essential and most
important element of leadership is the individual's passion or
conviction. Although I have already raised this point and will
explore it in much greater depth in Chapter Five, I will draw on
Janet Hagberg's work (2003) in this chapter to discuss the discovery of passion and conviction and to address the question of how
educators can help students learn how to mobilize innovation and
change.

Hagberg proposed that leadership was not just about our
positions or the power we wield but, instead, centered on the
"continual change and deepening we experience that makes a difference in our lives, our work, our world" (p. 273). Her metaphor
of leadership as a journey emphasized that the real opportunities
begin when we become frustrated with our own leadership. This
path involves delving into our fears, abandoning control, and freeing ourselves to find new inner strength informed by moral passion.
Through these freeing experiences, we can express leadership with
fresh perspectives and provide the unencumbered innovation that
is so deeply needed to achieve change.

Core Findings

Hagberg advocated soul leadership and described it as involving
the discovery of "meaning, passion, calling, courage, wholeness,
vulnerability, spirituality, and community" (p. 274). The following characteristics of soul leaders were deemed most important to
unleashing creative potential: knowing what it meant to be part
of or to create community; acknowledging vision as coming from
others as well as from themselves; giving power away; maintaining a sense of peace even in chaos; practicing integrity, reflection,
and collaboration; exhibiting humor and creativity; and show-
ing courage. These attributes freed the soul leader as well as fostered a climate that invited others to contribute. In essence, all

participants were allowed to be themselves, to express their views freely and openly, and to offer novel perspectives and talents.

Hagberg suggested several ways to develop soul leadership potential. Among them were three that seem most directly related to drawing out the potential for greater innovation: experiencing regular solitude in order to quiet one's external life, trying a new artistic endeavor, and escaping the safe and familiar. She also proposed six recommendations to pursue inner healing and transformation to open the way for the soul leadership journey. These included taking spirituality seriously, finding a mentor different from oneself, finding peace and intimacy in relationships without avoiding the natural conflicts within them, embracing the shadows and wounds that hold one back, discovering one's passion, and accepting one's calling. Regarding the last item, she noted that in leadership we are called to be faithful to ourselves and our purposes, not to be successful. This may seem odd in a discussion of leadership, but Hagberg's point was that if our purposes are authentic, success will find its way or another path will emerge.

Soul leadership may seem an unusual pathway to innovation. However, we only have to reflect for a moment to realize that hurried, routine, controlling, and predictable circumstances squelch our creativity and willingness to explore new possibilities. The soul leader is centered, freed, and capable of freeing others for the challenging work of innovation.

Implications and Use

Soul leadership is perhaps one of the most important foundations for the new leaps and advancements that will create the marketplaces, communities, and organizations of the future. Leadership based on this perspective must let go of conventional views of leading that are based on structured, bureaucratic organizations. Familiar and predictable environments tend to reinforce comfortable notions of how organizations function and thus encourage routine over modernization. One way to spark creativity is to explore an entirely different experience or idea and then try to make connections that are novel and out of the ordinary. An example might be to visit a modern art museum on campus or in the region. Modern art is by definition new, different, and outside the historical conventions of art. A trip to such a gallery would expose students to new conceptions of art. Well-designed modern art buildings are usually art in themselves. As students browse galleries, they should be encouraged not only to look at specific pieces of art but also to consider how the various pieces interact, how their display influences viewers' perceptions of the art, and how the building housing the art raises new awareness in itself. Turning a corner and viewing an open window on a garden can be as artistic as the Monet mounted on the far wall.

Going to new artistic, historic, or scientific environments can stimulate rethinking various issues of leadership. How are guests to a gallery welcomed and introduced to the experience that awaits them? How and why are we drawn into some spaces and not others? What is it about spatial arrangements that allow us to breathe and take in our surroundings as opposed to others that stifle, confuse, or overwhelm us?

Such metaphorical or experiential learning requires preparation and debriefing. Students would need to be asked what they antici-pate from such an experience and, more important, be challenged to reflect after such an encounter. Reflecting could be accomplished through writing, discussion, a visual representation, or other activi-ties. The important point is that these experiences should be used as a stimulus for students to translate the experience (whatever it may be) to their leadership and community involvement.

Another more direct way to explore soul leadership is to draw students' spiritual journeys into the study and development of lead-ership. Some institutions, most notably those that are public, avoid relating any curricular or cocurricular programs to spiritual questions. Unfortunately, this disregards the great importance of spiritual explo-ration in students' lives. Especially when focused on the discovery of conviction and passion in our lives, leadership learning will inevitably flow into broadly defined notions of spirituality. Leadership educators need to be prepared to embrace and use these opportunities.

The Making the Match research and the gaps it identified in college and university education framed two broad areas that I proposed for consideration in leadership learning: managing people and tasks and mobilizing innovation and change. Even when we are aware of the gaps and have models to help higher education improve its effectiveness in these areas, two important questions remain: How do college students come to see their own potential in leadership? How do students discover the leadership questions most needing their attention?

Leadership Identity Development

Leadership educators know that it is a given that in any group of students there are those who see themselves as leaders and others who do not. Some students strongly assert that they either are or are not leaders, whereas others appear more uncertain about their leadership abilities. The difference between those who identify themselves as leaders and those who do not was the question explored by Komives, Owen, Longerbeam, Mainella, and Osteen (2005).

The Leadership Identity Development model resulted from using a grounded theory method to explore thirteen diverse students' views of leading and leadership. The method of study included three successive interviews exploring the subjects' life histories, their experience with groups and leadership, and how their views of leadership had changed over time. The objective of the study was to determine a progression in students' leadership identity or capacity around which leadership programs and learning could be designed.

Komives et al. (2005) found that subjects in the study shifted from hierarchical and leader-centric views to more collaborative and relational views. Leader-centric views focused on individuals in positional and authoritative roles. Gradually subjects perceived a more interdependent world, which resulted in a leadership-differentiated view that recognized leadership more as a process than one personified in an individual. Those subjects who eventually recognized the systemic nature of leadership were categorized as in the generativity or integration or synthesis stages of the Leadership Identity Development model.

Adult and peer influences, meaningful involvement, and reflective learning formed the core of influences, or a type of holding environment, that shaped students' views of leadership. The degree and type of impact that these variables had on leadership learning changed depending on where subjects were in their leadership identity development. Two areas were found to interact with one another and eventually impact subjects' changing views of themselves and others: developing self and group influences. Developing self had subparts of deepening self-awareness, building self-confidence, establishing interpersonal efficacy, applying new skills, and expanding motivations. Group influences included the subparts of engaging in groups, learning from membership continuity, and changing perceptions of groups. As developing self and group influences interacted, subjects' views of themselves moved from dependent to independent and eventually to interdependent. These changing views contributed to a progressive and broadening view of leadership beginning with external other (others are leaders but not me) to positional (those who have titles and authority are leaders), then from positional to include positional and nonpositional, and finally from positional and nonpositional to leadership as a process. This broadening view became more inclusive as it progressed. Therefore, at the last level, a variety of types of leadership, reaching all the way from authority and power to shared and mutual influence, were recognized as possible and were observed in self and others.

Komives and her colleagues determined that the interaction of these several experiences and subjects' unfolding understanding of themselves constituted a leadership identity. This identity progressed through six stages: awareness, exploration and engagement, leader identified, leadership differentiated, generativity, and integration and synthesis. Awareness involved observing or recognizing leadership. During this stage, subjects perceived significant role models as leaders, but these leaders were external to the subjects' own identities. In the exploration and engagement stage, subjects took initiative and responsibility as followers or members. The leader-identified stage resulted in the subjects seeing specific individuals, either themselves or others, as playing roles of leader and follower. During the fourth stage, leadership differentiated, subjects moved away from viewing specific persons as leaders and began to recognize leadership as a process exhibited by numerous people. In the generativity stage, subjects made active commitments to initiatives and causes and then sought to develop individuals and teams to work toward a common purpose. The last stage, integration and synthesis, represented a channel or conduit to lifelong learning in leadership. At this stage, the subjects expressed a constant striving toward greater confidence, congruence, and eventual integrity in leadership. Dissonance in one stage in the Leadership Identity Development model caused subjects to adapt to another stage, thus moving to a different view of leading or leadership. Alternatively, new views of themselves and the groups within which they worked stimulated a different concept of leadership. The transition from stage three, leader identified, to stage four, leadership differentiated, was one of the most important as it marked the movement from seeing individuals as leaders (leader-centric) to the view that leadership could be shared, episodic, and collaborative.

The Leadership Identity Development model represents a break-through toward understanding students' progressive experiences with leadership. As additional research and exploration of these ideas appears in print (Komives et al., 2006), it will become easier to address students' perceptions of their leadership capability as it changes over time and experience. In practice, the model helps educators realize that students who arrive at a program or class believing that certain individuals are more capable of leading than others probably have not been exposed to the evolution of leadership thought and are just beginning to develop their identity in terms of leadership. An awareness of the interaction between group influences and the development of self, and of how these contribute to progressively broadening leadership views, become powerful tools for guiding students along the pathway of understanding more complex and inclusive leadership models.

The emerging understanding of how students' leadership identities may differ and evolve raises the question of what kinds of experiences, encounters, and processes could support and challenge them as they move through this progression. One of the theories that has been most influential in leadership learning and has specific pedagogical methods to demonstrate and teach it is adaptive leadership.

Adaptive Leadership

Ronald Heifetz's *Leadership Without Easy Answers* (1994) asks us to address leadership as it is informed by the nuance and dynamics of the group. He referred to two broad categories of leadership: technical and adaptive. Heifetz defined technical leadership as doing what was required to address an issue or problem when there was a known or knowable resolution. Adaptive leadership worked best when the solution was unknown and participants had to be drawn together to discern a new pathway. Technical leadership was more direct than adaptive leadership and was clearly more comfortable for organization members. In fact, it was so comfortable that members frequently sought a technical solution even when an adaptive response was more appropriate. For example, in a student organization context, technical questions related to participation would include what could be done to achieve more visibility on campus and which marketing and promotion methods would get the organization name out more effectively. An adaptive leadership question would refer to the organization's perceived or real values and how they can be promoted in a way that is of compelling interest to students. Essentially related to public relations, the technical question and response might achieve some gain. However, the issue of how to best promote the organization could be resolved within the organization's resources. Exploring the core values and purposes of the organization requires a deeper level of leadership and adaptive challenges, and it is on these challenges that Heifetz focused his attention.

Heifetz warned that there were a number of perils involved in adaptive leadership, because such challenges require experimentation, the discovery of new knowledge, and various adjustments throughout the organization. Only by adjusting attitudes, values, and behaviors could participants adapt to a new environment and sustain such change over time; this shift in values or perspective was the most difficult. For change to occur, participants had to be disloyal to their past and some of the constructs and relationships that shaped it. For example, if a student government were to consider abandoning formal organization processes such as resolutions, formal reports, and Robert's Rules of Order, they would have to be disloyal to the processes utilized in previous student governments, city councils, and even state and federal legislative bodies. Exploring new possibilities meant entertaining the prospect that current organization processes were ineffective. However, staying with the old way may have obscured the deeper and more important concern related to core organization purposes. Returning to the example of the student organization's participation, better public relations might help, but using a technical approach may also mask the more substantial change that could enhance the organization's effectiveness.

Heifetz noted that adaptive leadership was threatening to organizations and could elicit different forms of resistance. Marginalizing, diverting, and attacking were three strategies that organizations used to shut down adaptive change. These varied in the degree to which they represented overt or covert strategies, but they were relatively easy to spot as resistance. Another attempt that was less easy to identify was seduction or co-opting. In the co-opting strategy, members resisted adaptive leadership by incorporating it into the regular functions of the organization. An example could be when a grassroots change effort, such as a drive to purchase only clothing produced in work environments that pay a fair wage, was incorporated into the institutional purchasing process. Such a strategy would not necessarily undermine the effort but could slow or reduce the impact of a more active student boycott of sweatshop-manufactured clothing.

Another important lesson that Heifetz offered was that leaders frequently avoided or did not listen to those who disagreed with them. Heifetz recommended doing just the opposite. In order to refine one's own strategy and respond to the questions of adversaries, one needed to listen carefully to the reservations others expressed. Listening does not mean abandoning one's goal but does push one to become better informed of others' reservations and thus work more effectively for change.

One of the most frequently cited metaphors from Heifetz's work is the concept of going to the balcony. Adaptive leadership would be most effective when leaders gained objectivity and perspective by going to the balcony to observe the dance floor below. Many leaders failed because they could not see the patterns, nuances, and intricacies of what was going on around them. A skilled and adaptive leader would use one or more strategies to help regulate the tension presented in an organization facing adaptive challenges. The adaptive leadership response included (Heifetz & Laurie, 2001): direction (identifying the challenge and framing the issues); protection (letting the organization feel tolerable external pressures); orientation (challenging current or quickly emerging roles); managing conflict (exposing or letting conflict emerge); and shaping norms (challenging unproductive norms). These adaptive leadership responses gave the work back to the group and sought to engage members more fully so that the best responses could be identified. Only by managing the tension of adaptive leadership could leaders hope to secure the fullest and most helpful contributions from participants.

Another caution Heifetz and Linsky (2002) offered was that those who wished to lead needed to learn to manage their hungers. Hungers need not be avoided but simply managed. The primary hungers they identified were power, importance, and intimacy. Power could undermine adaptive leadership because the need to control and to direct would prohibit others from taking on adaptive work. The hungers for importance and affirmation bred heroic desires and behaviors that robbed contributors of the opportunity to develop their own strengths and resolve their own issues. Heifetz and Linsky proposed that the third primary hunger, intimacy, could result in seeking intimate company and relationships that would compromise effective leadership when left unchecked. There have been numerous public cases of leaders who have not managed their emotions, but the hunger for intimacy also routinely affects regular workplaces and communities where stress or loneliness cause leaders to turn to others for support and solace. Spreading office gossip and using confidants to vent about work frustrations are examples of sharing individuals' personal concerns that may reflect lingering hungers for intimacy.

The insights offered by Heifetz and his collaborators provide powerful lessons intended to help leaders maintain adaptive leadership commitments when appropriate. Falling into the resistance traps laid by others, not listening to those who disagree, losing objectivity, and falling prey to our hungers are all dynamics that can draw adaptive leadership away from its primary purpose: giving the work back to the groups and organizations we seek to lead.

Heifetz has perfected adaptive processes in his teaching. By creating course experiences that demonstrate the adaptive leadership variables he identified, Heifetz extended the relevance of the model while also providing guidance for those who wished to use the model in their own work. This Case-in-Point method has been described by Sharon Parks (2005) in great detail. This method of teaching provides the opportunity to use explicit and underlying issues in the group to demonstrate course content; thus the classroom becomes a studio for demonstration, performance, and experimentation. Although Parks described the teaching methods Heifetz used in a classroom setting, she offered insights that also hold relevance for cocurricular experiences. Most important, the Case-in-Point method enables the shift from positivist and heroic teaching to improvisational and artistic learning. Five elements—conscious conflict; pause; image or insight; repatterning; interpretation, testimony, and testing—form the core of both the artistic learning and leadership processes (Parks, 2005). Conscious conflict involves creating something new from what isn't working. Pause stimulates deeper thinking when the active mind is forced to step back. Image or insight occur when "aha" moments emerge, facilitating the resolution of conflict and students' abilities to interpret their own experiences. Repatterning results when previous assumptions are reconfigured in the light of new evidence. Bringing the new way of seeing and thinking to another party or group for confirmation or contradiction gives rise to the interpretation, testimony and testing phase.

Heifetz's adaptive leadership model and the Case-in-Point pedagogy that he has perfected provide bridges between the worlds of studying, critiquing, and practicing leadership. With skillful and deep preparation, educators can adapt the pearls of wisdom in Case-in-Point learning to a variety of settings. The adaptive leadership model also provided a link between the two broad areas that framed the theories we have explored in this chapter. The Making the Match research determined that the two broad gaps in what employers seek and what higher education prepares graduates to do are managing people and tasks and mobilizing innovation and change. Technical leadership, focused on how specific and knowable strategies guide a leader-centric group, results in a type of leadership that is more related to managing people and tasks. Adaptive leadership, focused on eliciting full participation from community members to devise previously unknowable responses to complex and difficult questions, is essential to mobilizing innovation and change.

Conclusions

I chose the models summarized in this chapter as a way to frame the questions of why deeper leadership should be cultivated and how this might be done. The twenty-first century presents massive change and uncertainty. Preparing college graduates to be effective in this changing world is one of the most compelling challenges we face in leadership learning. The Making the Match research by Evers et al. (1998) documented the need for college graduates who are more skilled in managing people and tasks and mobilizing innovation and change. The concepts of emotional intelligence introduced by Goleman et al. (2002) and soul leadership by Hagberg (2003) help us see how educators can encourage students to explore their inner purposes, reorient their compasses, and accept their calling in leadership and in life. Lipman-Blumen's connective leadership (1996) and Moss-Kanter's confidence (2004) offered deeper insight into how groups function and how educators can enhance students' capacity for good and productive mutual work. To help students discover their calling, educators can draw on the Leadership Identity Development model (Komives et al., 2005), which presents students' progression as they move from seeing leadership as embodied in external others to seeing themselves as capable of and involved in leadership. The Leadership Identity Development model highlights the shift in students' sense of efficacy and purpose when they began to discover their passions. The work of Goleman and Hagberg reinforced a similar belief about the importance of discovering passion and purpose. Lipman-Blumen and Moss-Kanter provided strategies for how those with conviction and purpose can respectfully engage others and invite them into connective and productive membership and leadership. Students' shift from leader-centric notions to shared and integrative forms of leadership are directly aligned with connective and confidence-building forms of organization leadership. Heifetz (1994) communicated the complexity of issues that require adaptive leadership responses as well as the methods that could help align partners' and participants' real work together with individual leader's convictions.

We have models to help us deepen leadership, but our dilemma is to understand the many available models and determine in which settings and conditions they could be most useful. I have not presumed to provide an exhaustive summary of new leadership theories in this chapter. My hope is that these interpretations and applications will stimulate new connections that you can explore with your colleagues and students.

5

Accessing Purpose and Voice
for Deeper Leadership

A challenging question facing educators and students of leadership is, "What theory or model will best serve my needs?" Regardless of whether your goal is to understand your own leadership potential or to design a leadership program that will impact others, your decision to select one model over another is subjective. Your own life experiences, your view of the world, and your interactions with those people who have been most influential in your life no doubt affect your choice.

Likewise, this chapter is subjective in that I present models that resonate with my personal experiences. It reflects my understanding of what deeper leadership could be—at this moment in time. My views have changed and have been refined throughout my life's encounters. As I have attempted to remain an active student of leadership, I have pooled the thoughts of numerous authors and added my own to develop a model that proposes the potential for a kind of leadership that digs down into the soul. I call this kind of leadership *deeper leadership*. I invite you to explore this model and its applicability to your own experience and I further request that you add your own experience to enhance the model's meaning.

Defining Leadership

I have heard hundreds of speakers, read thousands of articles and books, and engaged in countless conversations about the meaning of leadership. The variety of these perspectives frequently leaves me more confused than resolved. One moment in time presented the opportunity for me to focus, simplify, and discern what is for me a core and transcending idea. During that one moment in time, I sat among 400 college students eager to learn how to be better leaders. The students' casual chatter during the opening session of the leadership conference filled the auditorium with energy. The conference keynote speaker strode to the microphone and started his remarks with the question, "How many of you out there know what leadership is?" I was startled by the simplicity of the question, and I was unnerved by the fact that I was an experienced administrator in an audience of primarily undergraduate students. In this kind of setting, it was apparent that my life's work, study, and experience with leadership should have provided a clear definition. I hesitated for a moment, noticed that very few people in the room were raising their hands, and then took the risk to lift mine. By gift of providence, the keynoter did not call on me but, instead, asked for several students' opinions. In those moments of hesitation, and as I heard others speak of what they thought leadership was, I found an answer within myself that I had never explored before.

This wonderfully pregnant moment spurred me to discern one of the simplest definitions of leadership I've ever seen. This definition is the one I propose for your consideration:

☞ *Leadership = Conviction in Action*

Conviction in action is at once simple and complex, and it encompasses seven assumptions:

1. *It is inclusive.* Conviction in action embraces the belief that individuals with positions of authority and influence are capable of leadership as well as a belief that many others make a difference in their communities, workplaces, and broader world without ever having been given any title whatsoever.

2. *It involves inner and outer work.* Conviction in action incorporates inner work in which leaders engage in self-reflection

as well as outer work in which leaders seek to serve others. If I have not looked carefully at the things I value most, then I have no source of power within that sustains my commitments and shapes my interactions with others.

3. *It results in action.* Leadership is not only about thinking but includes taking steps to act on our convictions. If I intend no particular action now or in the future, how can I claim to be involved in leadership?

4. *It is based on honesty and openness.* Conviction in action provides an opportunity for me to share my views, without the need to manipulate or spin an idea to secure the acquiescence of others.

5. *It fosters courage.* Conviction is essentially the ability to overcome doubt, to be convinced that what I believe is achievable.

6. *It sows seeds.* Conviction in action serves as a catalyst for others' aspirations. When I express my convictions, I plant seeds of possibility or understanding in others' minds.

7. *It creates connections.* Conviction in action fosters mutuality. As a person who has deep convictions, I am so passionate about my beliefs that I will listen more deeply to others and will seek to help others achieve their purposes while at the same time enrolling them in mine. The process of exchanging and incorporating conviction then allows the synergies of purpose to unfold and thus enables me to achieve my goals while others achieve theirs.

This disarmingly simple definition, leadership = conviction in action, is related to and is derived from many other theories, all of which were noted in Chapters Three and Four. However, its simplicity makes it different from the many definitions that leadership educators and scholars debate and advocate. The reason I propose so simple a notion is to provide a way to start with agreement rather than hair-splitting critique over many words. My proposal is that by starting simply with a broad definition, to which you add your own meaning and rich perspective, we will be better able to recognize our commonalities rather than our differences in perspective.

The remainder of this chapter will address some of the concerns that are no doubt already beginning to flow through your mind. How can I find a source of conviction that lasts? How do I know that my conviction is worth pursuing? What if the convictions of someone else are contrary to my own beliefs? What if the expressed conviction has an intentionally negative impact on others or on the world? How can I always be "on" and consistent with my convictions? These questions and others will be addressed in the unfolding deeper leadership model to follow. First, I explore the origins of conviction and then draw on several existing theories and models to identify three paths—presence, flow, and oscillation—that lead toward deeper leadership.

Exploring the Conditions That Arouse Conviction

Leadership based in conviction is derived from personal awareness and reflection on the possibilities of the work worthy of our time and commitment. The kind of conviction that lasts, or provides the foundation for future discovery, is a journey toward an ultimate purpose or perhaps a vocation. Some trace the discovery of conviction to spiritual or other revelations in their lives. The difficulty is knowing where to start—especially for those who are younger or lack the kind of exposure to the world that stimulates questions of deeper purpose. We need not feel as if we must wait for divine inspiration or a life-changing experience to discover conviction. Sometimes, conviction stems from an ordinary observation coupled with the recognition of a compelling need. For example, one student whose leadership journey I've followed carefully noticed as a high school senior that promotional pharmaceutical pen supplies were being thrown away by his family physician at the same time he knew that there were people in Africa who desperately needed writing utensils to meet their basic educational needs. He started by asking that a box be provided in which nurses could place the supplies that they would typically discard. Within a short time, the first box was full, other boxes filled, and a shipment of 760 pounds of supplies was off to Africa. When this student entered college, he established a student organization to raise awareness of educational problems in Africa, and he delivered over $2,000 and a thousand pounds of educational supplies during his summer break. His next realization was that the organization he had founded needed to foster shared leadership among its members so that others could lead in his place, guaranteeing that the organization would eventually become sustainable after his graduation. In this small example, we see the seeds of discontent that led to modest possibilities at first and eventually grew into a major commitment, transforming awareness of the need into action to provide educational and medical supplies for people who desperately need this help. The origin of conviction is most likely a small step but one that has the potential to lead us toward finding and living out our authentic purpose.

Discovery of conviction among women who engaged in profound social change leadership mirrored the previous example. After studying the motivations and behaviors of seventy-seven women across three generations who had emerged into visible leadership roles, Astin and Leland (1991) concluded, "What becomes clear here is that leaders emerge from the critical interplay of personal values and commitments, special circumstances or historical influences, and personal events that motivate and mobilize people's actions" (p. 66). They discovered that the emergence of purpose varied among their subjects, just as it would be likely to unfold in students' lives. "Sometimes the development was intense and sudden, at other times it was gradual, and often it came with nagging reluctance" (p. 76). Understanding that conviction comes at different times and through different processes may unnerve some who would prefer a more predictable pattern. However, the uniqueness of the individual journey toward purpose reminds us that although there may be similarities among stories of conviction, we need always to acknowledge and affirm the personal work we each must undertake.

A troubling aspect of conviction is that it can be manifest in both good and bad leadership. This is one of the most difficult philosophical questions faced by those who seek to understand leadership: that leaders can be bad and can profoundly and negatively affect millions of people, environmental systems, and the very stability of life.

I used to dismiss bad leaders by rationalizing that they weren't really leaders. The way I constructed this in my own thinking was that leadership had to be only a positive act, one that influenced living conditions and circumstances of others in ways that enhanced rather than detracted from their quality of life. Discussions of Adolf Hitler's Nazi ideology and abuse are almost always part of any conversation on leadership. You can do as I did, which was to claim that he really was only a manipulator, a demagogue, a coercive agent of evil. Or you can recognize that there might have been in Hitler those moments when he actually displayed leadership capacities that many of us would embrace. The difference is in the ultimate outcome of what he did. Regardless of moments when Hitler may have displayed leadership, he caused immeasurable pain, agony, and devastation. He destroyed people and systems that stood in the way of his aspiration to dominate others absolutely.

Books by Jean Lipman-Blumen (2004) and Barbara Kellerman (2004) on toxic and bad leadership convinced me to recognize that leading can have very negative qualities. Furthermore, recognizing bad leadership and toxic leaders allowed me to get on with the important work of understanding how leadership is exhibited for both positive and negative purposes. Kellerman in particular identifies leaders who ranged from ineffective to unethical. To some extent, it doesn't matter whether the leadership style falls under the category of ineffective or unethical; each style has negative repercussions. The continuum that Kellerman suggests includes incompetent, rigid, intemperate, callous, corrupt, insular, and evil. It is relatively easy to see how each of these forms of leadership can result in negative, or in some cases, tragic consequences.

Ineffective leadership, or a lack of developed leadership capacity, may be easier to address than unethical leadership. By drawing in others who could be more effective, leadership educators can help those who have a good purpose but are just bungling the opportunity. Or we can attempt to address the incompetence or rigidity, such as in training individuals in communication skills or helping them understand important skills of time or meeting management. Intemperance and callousness are deeper and more difficult to address; such leadership would more likely originate from a lack of exposure to and understanding of others. This kind of leadership may also be the result of repeated struggles in dealing with a problem or dynamic of groups. However, there is still opportunity to intervene in such a situation to help individuals and organizations become more patient or responsive.

By contrast, ill intent is a much more difficult problem. Corrupt, insular, and evil leadership is malignant in its purpose. Corruption and insularity are frequently based on arrogance, disconnection, and a mentality of "my way is the right way." There is little room for learning when these forms of leadership are present. Those who have ill intent may be misinformed, unaware, or biased. Or ill intent may come from deeply rooted purposes—those that seek to demean, discredit, diminish, or eliminate others.

If we assume that ineffectiveness can be resolved through a number of strategies, then what could we do about the truly evil intent, especially when that evil purpose is not immediately recognized by others? Here we can attempt to intervene with the person or people exhibiting destructive leadership, hoping that we can influence them to see how their leadership is negatively impacting others. Or we can urge those who are intentionally or inadvertently supporting destructive leadership to recognize it and formulate resistance to its toxic influences. Regardless of which intervention is available to us, the point is that others must recognize the negative leadership, confront it, and cease to tolerate its use.

The sad truth of my own experience is that I know that there are examples of when I have aided and abetted bad leadership. By not confronting others, I have contributed to their success. Even worse, as a leadership educator, I have to admit that I have helped a few bad leaders to acquire the skills to be successful in their leading. I had hoped to improve the core of these individuals and to help them realize the ethical and service aspects of their lives, but in reality I have only helped them improve their communication skills or their ability to "spin" their message to obscure the destructive reality of their purposes. That I have ignored bad leadership or inadvertently assisted in making it more effective is a sobering realization.

To determine whether and how to challenge bad leadership, I have found that the best test is to challenge myself and others to explore the purposes and convictions of leadership. Why is it that you or I want to acquire a specific role or position? What do we intend to accomplish by gaining agreement to our proposed action? Who is best served by the project on which we want others' support? These are the kinds of questions that can begin to open the door to understanding that allows us to recognize and confront bad leadership.

Ultimately, one of the most valuable means of cultivating effective and constructive leadership is to look at core purposes. Examining core purposes can reveal the transformative potential that can be found in serving others. Authentic purpose or conviction will result only when those of us seeking to provide leadership recognize the wholeness of the interconnected world in which we live. There are many worldwide notions of this relationship, but one that conveys this most effectively is the idea of *ubuntu*.

☞ *Ubuntu = Commitment to Wholeness*

The African concept of *ubuntu* affirms the organic wholeness of humanity. The notion is enshrined in the Xhosa proverb *umuntu ngumuntu ngabantu,* meaning "a person is a person through persons"

(Villa-Vicencio, 1996, p. 298). This belief recognizes the presence of the divine in others and asserts that we are shaped for good and bad by all those with whom we share our lives. A rough translation in English of the concept of *ubuntu* is "humanity towards others," or the "belief in a universal bond of sharing that connects all humanity." In the words of Archbishop Desmond Tutu (2005), "A person with *ubuntu* is open and available to others, affirming of others, does not feel threatened that others are able and good, for he or she has a proper self-assurance that comes from knowing that he or she belongs in a greater whole and is diminished when others are humiliated or diminished, when others are tortured or oppressed." Ideas similar to *ubuntu* can be found in such diverse world traditions as Buddhism, Judaism, Christianity, Islam, Tao, and in nonreligious perspectives such as secular humanism and generosity or abundance beliefs.

If leaders hold core convictions like those described above—believing in the interconnectedness among humans, nature, and the systems that sustain us—then they are much more likely to be worthy of trust. Indeed, when we trust in the belief that we are all connected and that our welfares are intertwined, our behaviors toward one another change. We become more aware of one another, more responsive, flexible, centered, and committed to contribute to the common good—qualities that are just the opposite of what Lipman-Blumen and Kellerman helped us to see as the characteristics of bad leadership.

If leadership is conviction in action, and core purposes are formulated in relation to the benefit and welfare of the whole, we have a significant start in understanding the kind of leadership that is worthy of trust and is worth our effort to cultivate. What is the process that could result in the kind of depth and personal reflection that would make this possible?

Discovering the Paths Toward Deeper Leadership

In this section, I propose that if we are to discover and live a life in which leadership becomes a process of acting on our convictions and positively contributing to the advancement of the human condition, we need to include the exploration of presence, the maintenance of flow, and the oscillation of experience. These three concepts allow for renewal of creativity and energy in making a difference. The three "paths" are necessary to move toward deeper leadership, leadership shaped by purpose that allows for renewal throughout life's experience.

Integrating Personal Reflection and Social Action

The first path, presence (Senge, Scharmer, Jaworski, & Flowers, 2004), involves moving through six broad stages that include seeing, sensing, presencing, envisioning, enacting, and embodying. Senge et al. describe an unfolding process that they shared as authors and that led them to recognize this six-stage progression. Exhibit 5.1 illustrates the Presence model.

Exhibit 5.1: Presence Model

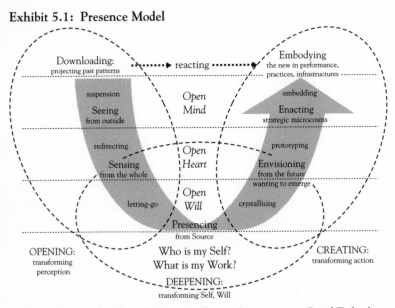

Note: From *Leading from the Emerging Future: Presencing as a Social Technology of Freedom* (in press), by C. Otto Scharmer. See also http://ottoscharmer.com. Used by permission.

In the next several pages I will explain what seeing, sensing, presencing, envisioning, enacting, and embodying are and how these steps unfold in relation to deeper leadership. Some of these words, particularly "presencing," may not hold much initial meaning for you. Once you are more familiar with the words, you are likely to see their intuitive relevance and meaning, and that their most important use is in reflecting on others' and your own experiences in discovering and acting on conviction.

A very important underlying belief of the Presence model is that those who move through it experience a gradual opening of mind, heart, and will. Open mind, open heart, and open will are in the center of Exhibit 5.1 to portray the deepening journey of discovering purpose in life. Cultivating an open mind allows us to consider other information, perspectives, and evidence of which we were unaware or that we previously ignored. The preparatory step of downloading preconceived notions opens the way for us to see the world around us in a more descriptive, accurate, and complete way. This opens our minds so that new information can be absorbed. An open heart follows from an open mind when we begin to sense new ways of viewing and relating to the world around us. Sensing is enhanced not only by information but by an emotional intuition about things that might be. As our hearts are opened, the reality of others' life experiences and circumstances begins to pry on our conscience and, indeed, pushes us to consider changing the way we view and act toward them. At the deepest point of Exhibit 5.1 we see presence, which comes from an open will to do something about what we have begun to see and sense. As our will opens, we see the possibilities presented by changing our views, our commitments, and our actions. Open will is the foundation for presence, or being present in, the work of deeper leadership. Keep open mind, heart, and will in mind as I describe these phases in greater detail.

Downloading

The six stages of the Presence model characterize a deeper level of reflection and analysis than is typical of many of our life experiences.

Much of what we do in life is out of habit—it's familiar and routine. The process involved in presence requires first that we erase the slate of our previous awareness. The beginning of the path to presence requires discarding previous notions that could restrict a deeper and more informed understanding of the world and the conditions in which we live. The initial process, which Senge et al. term intellectual or emotional downloading, functions much like a computer where data or documents are placed on the "desktop," or temporary memory, of our awareness. I think of this as ridding myself of conventional or prescriptive notions that could inhibit deeper understanding. By doing so, previous notions remain on the desktop, kept out of the way so that I can acquire new understandings by looking carefully at the current environment and conditions that surround me. Downloading doesn't mean denying our previous notions; rather, we choose to suspend the conclusions while we explore other insights.

Seeing

Downloading clears the way for the first stage of the Presence model: seeing. In the seeing process, we begin to focus on circumstances and conditions that we may previously have not seen. The blur of daily existence is removed. The cataract that made it difficult to focus no longer inhibits our clear vision of the circumstances before us. During the seeing process, we are also able to get outside of our own frames of reference. If our life experiences constrict seeing the world anew, downloading and seeing provide the opportunity to gain perspective or distance. The combination of seeing both more detail and seeing more broadly sharpens our vision and provides the foundation for the next stage: sensing. Our minds are open to new possibilities.

Sensing

Sensing is the beginning of the call to leadership. Seeing detail and context at the same time allows us to see from the whole, rather than just from our own previously narrow view. An open heart is critical at this point. Responding to the call of leadership requires us to let go—of other things we could have done, of freedom, of leisure. When I become convinced of the need to take leadership, I feel as if a magnet is drawing me toward a project (or purpose). I feel the angst of concern or dissatisfaction that compels me to act. It's as if I have no choice but to do something.

After we feel compelled to act, we need to find ways to break down false illusions so that we can see the true challenges that we need to address. Life experiences result in many illusions about the circumstances around us. For instance, we may see homeless people in the street asking for help; yet, the illusion we have is that this is their choice. "If they wanted help, it's available through governmental or private programs" would be one way we may dismiss the plight of a real person whom we encounter. We discover that such a belief is an illusion only when we are willing to experience the phenomenon we observe. In order to explore whether programs are or are not available to help the homeless, one might actually go into the streets to spend time with the homeless, talk to them, ask them for their view of life and how they came to be homeless. Taking the risk to actually engage with others more deeply provides the opportunity for disillusionment, an important step to being able to sense new possibilities.

Presencing

When seeing and sensing give way to presencing, we are subject to very powerful forces. The open mind and heart give way to an open will that calls us to act. Presence is what many of us see as authenticity in others or the "just being real" that is so attractive. People who are present have an unusual power in their interactions. Consider the actor or public figure whose "presence" was so notable. After a great theater performance, we frequently comment that an actress had such amazing stage presence. This is exactly the kind of real and compelling feeling we get when we are around someone who is present in their leadership. We know that we will not have to guess where they stand. Their commitments are obvious and they will work tirelessly to communicate their purposes while respecting those of others.

The beauty and attractiveness of leadership based on presence is that we know it can be trusted, because of its honesty and forthrightness. We know that this form of leadership is not arrogant and will not risk the imposition of will on others because presence involves the expression of will in another very powerful way—through listening to others and engaging with others in the discovery of common ground and mutual benefit. In describing Ron Heifetz's Case-in-Point teaching method, Sharon Parks (2005, p. 100) addressed presence when she said, "The elusive quality of presence affects one's ability to attract and hold attention, to convey trustworthiness and credibility, to inspire and call forth the best in others, to intervene effectively in complex systems, and to be a conduit of creative change." "This is my work" is the ultimate conclusion for individuals who reach this level of awareness and depth. It doesn't mean that there won't be other work to do at other times or that things will never change. What it does mean is that there is intensity in leadership that allows us to proclaim what we stand for. Even individuals who more often may be quiet observers will be comfortable in proclaiming their purpose and engaging with others to accomplish it. Discovering conviction empowers us all to take leadership in creating a better world.

Because presence is difficult to discern, an example may be useful. There are few public figures of whom I can be assured we are all aware, but former President Jimmy Carter is probably someone whom we mutually know on the basis of his reputation. Carter was not necessarily seen as among the greatest presidents the United States has ever had; yet I've heard it said that Jimmy Carter was the only president in modern times who used the presidency as a stepping-stone to greater accomplishments. What an amazing statement this is, as many citizens of the United States and elsewhere would perceive being president of the United States as a pinnacle accomplishment. Jimmy Carter left a position of authority to use his personal influence, his conviction, and his presence to cultivate awareness of the possibility of peace in the Middle East. Jimmy Carter has also served as an advocate to rectify the problem of substandard housing around the world through his work on behalf of Habitat for Humanity. In addition to speaking, he has contributed his time, resources, and sweat toward building houses for those in need. When you see Jimmy Carter in person or in the media, you see the same person. If you have a chance to listen to him carefully, you hear only very authentic and worldcentric concerns coming from his communication and actions. Regardless of political persuasion, most individuals recognize that during his term in office and afterward, former President Carter has reflected that he puts his conviction into action. This deeply felt, authentic action is exactly what we see as the presence of deeper leadership.

Envisioning

When we engage with others around purposes we care about, these new ideas stimulate us to envision a changing world. Senge and his colleagues propose a process of envisioning as the means to define a shared vision. Envisioning involves gathering ideas and resources to achieve what we seek: the vision. As these new ideas begin to crystallize, leadership is very tenacious, but not in a way that pushes its vision on others. The energy of individuals who know what they want is contagious and part of its contagion is that they are interested in others and in connecting with the aspirations of anyone they can find. Returning to the example of Habitat for Humanity, the idea of eliminating substandard housing sounds like an insurmountable goal, especially when we reflect on areas of urban blight or rural degradation we might have seen. However, if we have seen what it's really like to live in a dilapidated structure, perhaps lacking electricity, water, and other modern conveniences, an urgency or angst about the fact that so many people live in these conditions may compel us to act. The problem is, even if we have deep conviction about wanting to do something, many problems like this are so big that we avoid allowing this consciousness to emerge in our minds and hearts. One of the ways of overcoming the inertia of inaction is to accept that we don't have all the answers that will resolve substandard housing. Instead, we believe so deeply that it must be resolved that we will do anything to begin to make progress.

To envision is to have a picture of how something might be. It is having a different idea in our head about how a particular circumstance might be if it could be improved. Envisioning includes a process of discerning the future that wants to emerge, thus breathing new life into the possibilities that can be. As an example of the difference between observing and envisioning, consider what we know about hunger. Fifty years ago, many of us assumed that the population explosion around the globe would eventually result in mass starvation. Through various activist education efforts, we now know that the problem is not the quantity of food but its distribution. In fact, there is enough food on Earth to feed all people, if only we could conserve and use reasonably, and if we could find ways to distribute food resources around the globe to those in need. What keeps us from addressing global hunger is an assumption that it cannot be resolved and the lack of will to provide the human and economic resources to address the problem. If food distribution could be tackled, the next issue that would emerge is disproportionate population growth in those areas of the world where food is most scarce. More important, in many areas with scarce food resources, education is also poor. Envisioning a world without hunger would then have to include seeing food as abundant, finding ways to share it equitably, educating people in regions of high population growth about the importance of birth control, and seeking to lift the standard of living for all. Envisioning is the process of discerning a future seeking to emerge. With world hunger and many other problems, a holistic, complex, multifaceted, and shared vision must be created. This is the group process of envisioning an ideal future that can benefit all.

Enacting

Enacting, the next stage in the process, comes out of the envisioning experience. Enacting is most often demonstrated in small, initial and provisional steps. Returning to the dynamics of the envisioning experience, if we think of the changes we seek in too broad, sweeping, and pervasive a way, we may not even take the first step. The Presence model proposes that enacting is taking the initial steps to test the effectiveness of our strategies. Enacting may include taking microscopic steps to get us started. The microscopic advances serve as prototype attempts that allow us to refine our strategy as we work for bigger and broader change over time. The opportunity of working with college students through enacting steps are enormous. Most eighteen- to thirty-year-olds (or older) will not have the experience, resources, or wherewithal to address the conditions of the world about which they are concerned. However, collegians have always been characterized as inquisitive, seeking, restless, and willing risk takers. Helping college students enact provisional and pilot actions achieves several goals. First of all, enacting establishes a sense of "I can do something," or empowerment. As the first steps are taken, we either gain greater momentum from accomplishing something or we learn from our mistakes. When we are successful, even in small ways, we attract others to our cause. If we begin a fund-raising drive to address issues associated with substandard housing, we increase awareness among others, which leads to more funds and volunteers who come forward as they see the possibility of change. When enacting results in empowerment, ideas are refined, momentum builds, more partners are attracted, and a cycle of change is created. This is what enacting is all about.

Embodying

Embodying is incorporating the lessons learned through envisioning and provisionally enacting into the ongoing systems that will sustain the changes. Embodying could refer to personal, group, or organizational changes that represent true paradigm shifts in the way the broader dynamics operate. Embodying might be easiest to imagine when we think of individuals who have worked diligently for a transformative change over a long period of time. Often these individuals personify the change they seek. They are "the movement" or the vision because almost everything they say or do reflects back on the ultimate purpose. Mother Theresa is a good example of embodying, because it is so obvious that her focus was simply on service to others, not on bringing attention to herself. The result was that she represented a movement that brought critical medical, nutritional, and shelter assistance to the people of Calcutta. This is different from the individual whose leadership is driven by the desire for ego-gratification; it is usually easy to see through a motivation to be recognized for one's contribution versus recognition being the consequence of hard work and earnest effort. Recognition in the latter case may even be shunned because the person does not want to be singled out as responsible. By contrast, shared contribution and ownership is what is desired.

Before providing an example of how the progressive steps of the Presence model might unfold, let's look at another model that I summarized in Chapter Three. The Social Change model bears some striking similarities to the Senge et al. Presence model. It also helps to differentiate the work required of individuals from the work to be achieved collectively in the process of leadership.

As Exhibit 5.2 demonstrates, the process of leadership for social change proceeds from individual to group variables and is ultimately focused on an outcome of citizenship or engagement. The individual variables are not seen as sequential steps as much as they are variables that are critical considerations for leaders who work for social change as they reflect on the purposes in their work: consciousness of self and others, congruence, and commitment or conviction. Likewise, the group variables are not hierarchical but rather capture conditions that are optimal for effective work

Exhibit 5.2: Social Change and Presence

	SOCIAL CHANGE MODEL	PRESENCE
INDIVIDUAL VARIABLES	Consciousness of self and others	Seeing: Precise observation
	Congruence	Sensing: Tuning into emergent patterns
	Commitment and conviction	
GROUP VARIABLES	Collaboration	Presencing (discovering authentic presence): Accessing creativity and will
	Common purpose	Envisioning: Identifying new and different possibilities
	Controversy with civility	Enacting: Testing and prototyping change
OUTCOME	Citizenship	Embodying: Living the change

Note: Adapted from *Guidebook for a Social Change Model of Leadership Development,* by Higher Education Research Institute, 1996, Los Angeles: Graduate School of Education and Information Studies, University of California; and *Presence: Human Purpose and the Field of the Future,* by P. Senge, C. O. Scharmer, J. Jaworski, and B. S. Flowers, 2004, Cambridge, MA: Society for Organizational Learning.

in concert with others: collaboration, common purpose, and controversy with civility. The individual variables provide a base on which group conditions build. The result is trustable leadership based on authentic purposes and beliefs, transformed into group attributes that draw individuals and groups together. The result is collective action, or citizenship.

This exhibit reflects that the process involved in the discovery of purpose as described in the Presence model is parallel to the variables we see in the Social Change model. The beginning of the journey, seeing the world anew after discarding previous proscriptive notions of how it functions, is likely to involve a process of growing consciousness of self that contributes to greater congruence. Seeing requires that we introspect, take a critical look at ourselves and others, and pursue the internal work that allows us to be more congruent in who we are. Once we pursue this internal work, we can sense the possibility of things we would like to see changed in our world. In the Social Change model this is characterized as commitment or conviction.

Moving to the group variables of the Social Change model, we see collaboration and common purpose. The Presence model indicates that once we see the world more clearly and sense the possibilities of change, we begin to find our voice and to express our beliefs and aspirations. We are "present" with others when we collaborate and engage in true mutual work. Collaboration requires that there be a shared and common purpose among those working together. This is not coordination, sponsorship, cooperation, or other terms that sometimes pass for collaboration. The kind of collaboration referenced here is based on respectful and deep sharing of purpose.

One of the more interesting variables in the Social Change model is the last of the group variables: controversy with civility. A critical part of authentic and engaged group process is recognizing and welcoming the strife and struggle of different opinions. If groups are not able to sustain disagreements in healthy and constructive ways, they are very likely to miss essential elements necessary to success. Constructive disagreement is the critical thinking process personified in a group context.

In the Presence model, being present in the moment, accepting that others have different perspectives, listening carefully, and working toward an amenable shared perspective are essential in order to envision a shared strategy or solution. Envisioning and then acting in the moment through trial and error will take place most effectively when all participants feel valued and are willing to contribute diverse and important perspectives to the plan. Finally, enacting and embodying in the Presence model are precisely what happens when individual and group variables in the Social Change model take form through acts of citizenship. Citizenship does not only refer to acts of political engagement; this form of citizenship includes taking responsibility for our actions and being willing to invest ourselves in the collective good of our organization, community, or broader system.

An example may be useful to demonstrate how the Presence model and Social Change model might unfold in an act of deeper leadership in a student organization. The Kettering Foundation funded a project from 2002 to 2007 titled "Fraternal Futures." The project was conceived by educators as a way to draw students into taking responsibility for the conditions, environment, and future of fraternal organizations on college campuses. One of the primary reasons that this project was undertaken was that fraternal organizations had experienced considerable difficulty over at least the past five decades, resulting in many campuses and international headquarters imposing rules, practices, and programs on them. The imposed strategies were relatively easy to circumvent among creative undergraduates who were not involved in devising the solutions and did not support them. In essence, the changes initiated to reform fraternal organizations have been top-down edicts at worst and persuasion and incentivized manipulation at best (Roberts & Rogers, 2003). Considering the problems many campuses had with fraternal organizations, there seemed to be few alternatives.

At the heart of many of the difficulties facing fraternal organizations is that they have become something other than what their founders envisioned, but contemporary undergraduates in many cases simply don't see the problem. They joined these organizations for friendship, camaraderie, and social networks, and, in their thinking, who's to argue with that? Maybe there wasn't anything wrong with organizations that had such a purpose, as long as they abided by the law and did no harm to others. There is, however, one point of potential disconnect—fraternal organizations were not created only as places to meet friends and develop social networks. At their founding, fraternal organizations espoused a commitment to personal growth and development, scholarship, service, character, leadership, and brotherhood or sisterhood. Herein lies the problem: contemporary fraternal organizations had become something other than what they were intended to be.

In the fraternal organization problem, we see that there is a clear difference in perspective—what is seen as being appropriate or inappropriate in terms of the groups' purposes. The question was how to bring about change by helping undergraduates see a different potential purpose for these organizations, rather than imposing rules on them or cajoling them to make changes. The Fraternal Futures project (Roberts & Huffman, 2005) involved students in the creation of a deliberation model based on the National Issue Forum (NIF) process. The NIF model provided a way for citizens (in this case, students) to talk to each other and explore different perspectives on their organizations' purposes, and how these perspectives might be refined to serve their founders' purposes while still communicating a relevant message to contemporary college students. The Fraternal Futures deliberation involved peer-to-peer interactions that led to a clearer understanding of what was going on in these organizations. Once the group identified the complexities involved, the students began to deliberate in ways that helped them discern (that is, sense) the possibilities for a different and more productive future. Sensing new possibilities resulted in active, deeper discussions that fostered the will to change in individuals who then engaged with others to create a common purpose and collaborative strategies for change. The Fraternal Futures model accepts that there will be differences in opinion among the participants and that controversy in talking and planning for a new future is a positive outcome, not a problem to be feared. As individual students learned how powerful the founding ideals of their fraternal organization were, they developed a deep conviction about what must be done to protect their future, and they began to engage broader numbers of brothers and sisters in determining viable actions to bring about broad, systemic, and transformative change.

The Fraternal Futures initiative was also informed by the research and model building of Alan Berkowitz (1998), Richard Keeling (1998), and others who have conceived prevention work as a process of "social marketing." The strategy of social marketing addressed alcohol and other drug abuse, sexual assault, homophobia, and other campus problems, assuming that these problems resulted from misperceived norms of behavior. The Fraternal Futures deliberations involved students in deeper conversation about the history and purpose of fraternal organizations, corrected misperceived notions of such organizations as primarily social in their purpose, brought real problems to light, and encouraged students to see themselves as having influence and the ability to do something about their concerns. This work had demonstrable impact on students' views and confirmed that, when students are engaged in honest and real discussion and are given responsibility to make necessary changes, they step up to leadership responsibility. It also reflected the progression of seeing, sensing, presencing, envisioning, enacting, and embodying proposed in the Presence model and the individual and group development phases of the Social Change Model of Leadership Development.

The example provided here was very complex; it involved potentially thousands of voices and represented a formidable long-term change. The idea of presence is not one for the fainthearted, as it requires significant participation and commitment. A student leader seeking to make a difference in the fraternal world would need to perform long-term and deep work shared with many others—resulting in a living example of participation, engagement, and citizenship of the type needed in so many areas.

The concepts included in the Presence and Social Change models are confirmed by other theories. One of these models, described in William Perry's *Forms of Intellectual and Ethical Development* (1970), described nine stages of individual cognitive and ethical development through which young adults move as they mature. The other model, described in Ken Wilber's A *Theory of Everything* (2000), proposed "integral theory" as a way of understanding both individual and societal evolutionary phases. The following summaries of these two models will demonstrate how all four models relate to or confirm one other.

The Perry model was one of the most prominent developmental models used during the emergence of the student development movement in higher education in the late 1970s. It is a nine-stage model that can be collapsed into four broader phases: dualism, multiplicity, relativism, and commitment within relativism. The Perry model was originally based on research with undergraduate men at Harvard University in the 1960s, but subsequent research and applications of the model have demonstrated its relevance to women and to members of other culturally and intellectually diverse groups.

The first phase of the Perry model, dualism, is a phase typical of many undergraduates as they enter higher education. Students' thinking at this point is dogmatic, either-or, right-wrong, and dependent on authoritative perspectives. The person who has a dualistic perspective is intent on discerning the good authority who will shed light on the truth. There are good and bad authorities, and the good ones, with whom individuals in dualism identify, are those who can substantiate their perspectives with clear and conclusive rationale.

The second phase, multiplicity, is characterized by the realization that there may be other, perhaps many, relevant perspectives on any given issue. Students who exhibit this perspective are likely to see multiple views, but they still believe that there is one right way and that authority figures use multiplistic perspectives to either confuse or obscure the truth. Finding the truth may be conceived as an intellectual game for students who approach questions from a multiplistic perspective.

The third phase, relativism, discards the hope of a "right" or authoritative answer. In fact, students fully embracing relativism may become indignant to others' assertions of rightness. A kind of "anyone has a right to their own opinion" perspective pervades relativistic students' interactions and way of being.

The final broad phase, commitment within relativism, represents the point at which there is a realization that there are, indeed, multiple interpretations of a variety of life phenomena. Questions students might face as they begin to experience commitment within relativism range from determining the relevance of an academic theory to selecting a career to exploring matters of personal integrity. Within this relativistic stance, experience, evidence, and general patterns indicate that some perspectives are more defensible than others, some portrayals of phenomena more adequate than others, and some ways of thinking about certain areas of inquiry more useful and predictable than others. The Perry model conveys a movement from individualistic, noncontextualized understanding to views that recognize the relevance of others' views and finally to an acknowledgment of the need to develop diverse, interconnected, and mutually informing ways of seeing the world (Roberts, 1981).

Integral theory (Wilber, 2000) proposes that there is a natural evolution for us individually and collectively that can be observed and documented. This natural evolution or "Spiral of Development" serves as a map of interior and exterior consciousnesses. The three broad phases of this evolution are from egocentric to ethnocentric to worldcentric perspectives. In Wilber's proposal, evidence of movement through these phases is all around us and is expressed by different people and systems depending on the circumstances. The Spiral of Development can be broken into nine stages or memes: survival, kin spirits, power gods, truth force, strive drive, human bond, flex flow, whole view, and integral-holonic. At the early levels (survival, kin spirits, and power gods) we behave in very egocentric ways, demanding that our needs and desires be fulfilled, relying on instinctual and narcissistic behaviors to achieve our own individual or group goals. At the middle levels (truth force, strive drive, and human bond) these perspectives emerge: finding purpose, ensuring a future, and strategizing to prosper. There is a very strong ethnocentric bond among those seeking a shared future at the middle levels of the integral model; this results in the competitive, warring behaviors of groups that otherwise might be able to find common ground in their purposes. Wilber particularly notes the "green meme" thinkers, whom he critiques as progressive thinkers who hold back individual and societal evolution because they persist in judging others' perspectives as inadequate and ineffective for the world's present state. Wilber indicates that the final stages of the spiral (flex flow, whole view, and integral-holonic) are rarely seen in either history or the present. Fleeting moments of possibility thinking would include such activities as the drafting of the Constitution of the United States of America or Eleanor Roosevelt's advocacy for a statement on human rights. In the truly worldcentric view, there is a desire to integrate and align systems, to synergize, and to envelop all ways of thinking about the human condition. The final stages are integral in that they recognize, include, and make a place for all perspectives, rather than asserting the rightness of the world-centric notions. There may be a belief among those who perceive the world through worldcentric lenses that a particular course of action would be beneficial, but they continue to honor others' perspectives. This last point is very important because it represents a shift from integral theory's first to its second tier of thinking. In the first tier, some views seem right and others wrong, but the second tier recognizes that there are reasons why people and systems see things differently. The truly integral perspective advocates for the purposeful role of all forms of consciousness as a way to advance the evolution of individuals, groups, and systems.

The last phase of the Perry model is much like the worldcentric view (flex flow, whole view, and integral-holonic) of Wilber's integral theory. Both Perry and Wilber found few examples of the highest stages of their models. Both models propose that there is a time in individual development that embraces multiple possibilities. In these moments there is recognition that circumstances and evolution itself will likely result in integrated and synergistic belief systems and ways of viewing the world. The difference between Perry and Wilber is that Perry proposed his model as an individual developmental progression, whereas Wilber proposed integral theory as a process that can be seen in both individual and societal evolutions.

Sternberg (2007) reinforced the relevance of Perry's and Wilber's ideas when he advocated for the importance of wisdom in leadership. He even used specific terms such as contextualism and relativism to describe important capacities of effective leadership. His point was that the complexity and unpredictability of life require a broad and adaptive view of the challenges faced in leadership.

The Presence and the Social Change models propose ways of thinking about leadership that bring to the surface individual and group variables that are essential to deeper learning in leadership. The Perry and Wilber models introduce the challenge of how this deeper learning might be pursued. Much of the process of going deeper is developmental, but the remainder of the process includes experiences and other influences. It is fundamentally important not to use models like these as a way to critique anyone's place in life. We are where we are. Commitment within relativism (Perry) and second-tier thinking (Wilber) allow us to see the value of all places in the process of developmental evolution. The opportunity is to provide and explore more robust experiences that raise better questions throughout all levels and stages. Doing so will allow us to be successful in developing deeper leadership in ourselves and others. The goal is not necessarily to reach the "highest" levels or stages but rather to develop deeper leadership at whatever level or stage we find ourselves.

———————

The preceding discussions of presence, social change leadership, intellectual and ethical development, and the progression of human consciousness provide a foundation for understanding leadership as conviction in action. These models explore ideas and concepts that are beyond the consciousness of many of us at present, yet they propose ways of seeing the world that ideally are provocative and attractive. The models represent deep work that starts in the individual, is rooted in more critical and engaged opportunities to see the world in a realistic light, and involves authentic relationships. These authentic relationships are formed among people who bind together, although it is not always easy to do so, to address concerns that are recognized as common threats or conditions that need attention. This is intense work, and intensity requires a different kind of commitment, energy, and renewal. Two additional concepts that will help achieve intensity and renew it in deeper leadership are *flow* and *oscillation*.

Focusing Energy to Achieve Optimal Performance

The second path to deeper leadership, flow, is a concept coined by Mihaly Csikszentmihalyi (1993/2003). The idea of flow emerged from the study of peak performance and how those who achieve extraordinary levels of accomplishment are able to do so. Some of the groups studied were highly skilled surgeons, Olympic athletes, and great artists. Csikszentmihalyi's research found that human performance in almost any endeavor is at its highest when the focus is on achieving one's own best performance in the company of other high performers. In fact, seeking to be number one undermines high performance in some cases. When winning is all that counts, competition is less enjoyable and more stressful, and it comes with physiological and psychological barriers that negate what would otherwise be high performance potential.

The flow experience is made possible when individuals commit to pursue a dream and seek only to do the best they can do, considering their capability and the likelihood of achieving the dream. Exhibit 5.3 portrays the interaction of ability and perceived challenge as we work toward a goal.

As you can see, the least motivating environment is one in which both the challenge and skill expectations are low; this is referred to as apathy. Following the chart to the right from the apathy segment, increased skill or ability matched with continued low challenge results in boredom or relaxation. High skill and moderate challenge lead to a sense of control, a condition conducive to maintaining a current level of functioning but not calling forth the

Exhibit 5.3: Flow

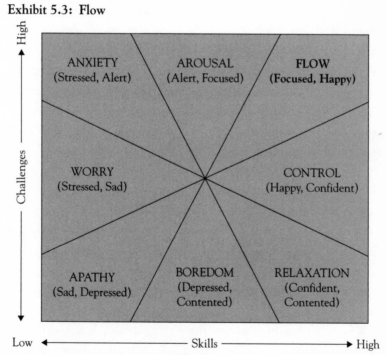

Note: Adapted from "Figure 2: The Map of Everyday Experience," in *Good Business,* by Mihaly Csikszentmihalyi, 2003. New York: Penguin. Copyright © 2003 by Mihaly Csikszentmihalyi. Used by permission of Viking Penguin, a division of Penguin Group (USA) Inc.

highest performance. Following the chart in the other direction, when skill level is low and the challenge increases, conditions of worry and anxiety are likely to occur. The optimal achievement possibilities exist when the challenge of a particular task is high and when skills are moderate (arousal), and especially when skill is high. This last combination, high challenge and high skill, is the "flow" segment that calls forth the highest intensity and optimal performance. Csikszentmihalyi's research indicates that the highest level of performance is achieved when the preparedness and ability are high and when the challenge is a little beyond anything we have ever achieved. In these circumstances, we push ourselves past the level of performance that we think would typically be possible.

What Csikszentmihalyi found among high performers who experienced this combination of high ability and high challenge is that they entered a state of flow. Flow is a heightened awareness and focus that blocks out everything but the goal. Another phrase sometimes used in athletic performance is being "in the zone." Long-distance runners, rowers, bikers, and athletes in other sports requiring intense and sustained focus lose track of time, space, and almost anything else around them. There is no time or attention left to be distracted. The same phenomenon was found among surgeons who could be in a four- to five-hour surgery and feel as if it were only fifteen minutes. Time passes effortlessly and without notice. Space and location can also be erased by a kind of tunnel vision that closes out peripheral sight. The level of concentration in flow is exhilarating. The task commands every ounce of our attention and energy, and it is this focus that allows us to maximize performance.

When driven by a compelling conviction, leadership can achieve a flow state where individuals and groups are able to achieve goals far beyond expected performance levels. We work harder, stay focused, don't let obstacles distract us, and draw the best out of all those around us. The conditions of flow include concentration, absorption, deep involvement, joy, and a sense of accomplishment. When these conditions are present, the activity becomes autotelic—worth doing for its own sake. Doing worthy work is self-sustaining and can overcome many blocks. The focus made possible in flow experiences draws us back to our original intent, even when there are circumstances or other people who stand in the way of accomplishing the goal.

The concept of flow also helps us understand how to turn competitive striving into productive performance. Misplaced competitive urges can undermine flow and peak performance by idealizing excellence for the wrong reasons. If we seek achievement only for its own sake, just to be recognized as the best, then our performance frequently falls short. However, if we seek to achieve simply for the joy of performance and for the pleasure of being in the company of other great performers, then we typically come closer to peak performance. The Latin derivation of *competition* is a combination of *con*, "with," and *petire*, "to search or seek." If we take this derivation literally, it means that competition requires others to achieve our personal best. It's not competition against others but with others that counts.

Leadership based on seeking a flow experience means living one's convictions, not as an act of will or competition, but as a compulsion to live at the edge of peak performance. We achieve flow by allowing ourselves to care deeply about the goal, striving for it with all our ability, maintaining focus, seeing that we are making progress, and enjoying every minute as we contribute our best effort. Flow provides a way for us to understand the power of focus and use it to organize and channel our time, talent, and resources.

Using Periods of Inactivity to Reflect and Rejuvenate

The third path, oscillation, was most succinctly described by Schwartz and Loehr (2001), although Parker Palmer (1990) has addressed the concept more elaborately in numerous speeches, articles, and books. Oscillation involves regular vacillation between periods of action and reflection. This vacillation allows for intense action and the reflective interlude during which we learn lessons from the prior experience and gather new energy to pursue the work with even more fervor at the next turn. If one is constantly engaged in action at a highly intense level, exhaustion, blurring, and inability to respond are likely to result. If one is minimally engaged or disengaged, high performance is never possible. With oscillation, highly intense and productive periods are possible, punctuated by periods of withdrawal for reflection and refocus.

Whereas flow offers the potential to focus and organize one's energy, oscillation provides the opportunity to disorganize it. Without disorganizing or disillusioning experiences, we can become so patterned and resistant to contrary evidence that we make mistakes. Reflection frequently results in our pondering questions that we've not considered before, realizing dimensions or implications of a question we didn't see, or more profoundly, discovering that the motivations we thought were pure and intended to help others were not that at all. Retreating to consider these possibilities can seem as if it is taking us off track but, in fact, taking the time for the reflective interlude helps to assure that we stay on track and that we pursue our goals for the right reasons. One of the easiest ways to see how this might be manifest is by looking at people who appear deeply committed to a humanistic and philanthropic project but manage to treat those working with them in ways that deny them their worth, dignity, and respect. How can an otherwise purposeful, caring individual demean those very individuals attempting to achieve the same goal? It's actually not very hard to fall into this trap, especially if regular oscillation between reflecting and acting are not a part of our routine discipline.

There are some interesting examples of forced withdrawal that allowed transformational potential to build in ways that have profoundly changed our world. It is fascinating to look at Martin Luther King Jr.'s time of imprisonment that resulted in "Letter from Birmingham Jail" (1964) or Nelson Mandela's imprisonment during apartheid that gave birth to the concept of reconciliation. These two examples of political incarceration created some of the most powerful social change moments in history. Little did King or Mandela's captors realize that they might be contributing to more powerful transformation potential by establishing the retreat necessary for new ideas and compelling visions to emerge. There are other examples of voluntary withdrawal, primarily seen among creative geniuses such as the composer Gustav Mahler and others who poured themselves into the creation of great music, art, and architecture. In the case of Mahler a studio served as his retreat for hours and days on end. If he was deeply engaged in a composition, he was emotionally unavailable to his friends and family even during times when he was not in the studio. Biographies of such artistic giants reflect repeated incidents of dry, barren, artistic waste punctuated by other periods of extremely high productivity and genius. It is almost as if the isolation were self-imposed or mystically applied so that gifted artists could bring such great insight to us in their work.

The other important aspect of oscillation is that none of us can maintain high levels of performance indefinitely. Intense work, focus, expenditure of physical and psychological energy—all of these require renewal. The down periods of oscillation allow us to regroup, rest, feed, and replenish the reservoirs that we have depleted through hard and diligent work. In many ways, our bodies are physiologically attuned to the need to replenish. Those who have work or leadership responsibilities that demand high energy and intensity may find that they collapse after challenging performance periods. The body knows its limits and will begin to shut down the mind and the psychic capability when the physical resources are exhausted.

Presence, Flow, and Oscillation—Paths to Deeper Leadership

Before providing summative reflections on the deeper leadership model that has been proposed in this chapter, it is important to note that accessing purpose and voice for deeper leadership is a subjective and personal model. You may find the model useful, but if it does not fit with your own experience, explore what does and then create strategies to work with colleagues and students in ways that create meaning for you and them. An individual or campus model must be unique and purposeful to the individuals involved and to the campus culture. Above all, this chapter proposed that some way of getting to ideas of deeper leadership was essential to the credibility of our commitments and programs in the years to come.

Combining the paths that have been described above will establish a foundation for the kind of leadership that is based in deep conviction. Presence allows for the discovery of something worth doing, flow encourages one to remain constant to the vision, and oscillation allows creativity and high performance.

Presence and cultivating it in ourselves and others is both developmental and cyclical. It is developmental because nurturing a deeper sense of knowing in ourselves requires taking the time to see the world more clearly, to sense the possibilities for change, to establish a core of conviction that allows us to be fully present in our living. Presence is also developmental in an organizational sense, stimulating organizations to see, sense, and proclaim new possibilities. Organizations are profoundly influenced by the dynamics of the Presence model when convictions move on to the stages of envisioning, enacting, and embodying that which we believe. Presence is cyclical because neither individuals nor organizations remain the same. We change as a result of beginning to see new perspectives or from achieving our goals. When this happens, presence becomes a tool to cycle back through phases of seeing, sensing, presencing, envisioning, enacting, and embodying. In some cases, the process of developing presence in ourselves and others becomes more familiar, allowing us to be more effective in this important work, or enabling us to recognize the journey and thereby pursue it more comfortably.

Flow allows leadership to be focused, purposeful, and intentional. When we pursue deep conviction, we expand individual and organizational capacity, mobilize resources, and break barriers in ways that we never imagined. Attention to recognizing and cultivating flow allows us to get into a deeper and more effective flow state more often. Flow is built on a focus that is clear and compelling, and we begin to organize our lives around it in ways that are very powerful.

Oscillation provides alternating periods of focus and purpose that disorganize and renew the work of leadership. The heightened state of flow directed at something of profound importance cannot be sustained indefinitely. Moments of retreat, relaxation, and renewal are necessary for us to make sure that our purposes are intact and that we have the energy reserve to do the job to the best of our ability.

Those of us inspirited by the call to make a difference in the world have no choice but to take the journey of self-discovery. We experience peak moments in leadership when we have anticipated but not yet realized a compelling vision of a possible future, when we are pushed to the maximum as we seek to achieve it, and when we are uncertain whether we will attain success. The transformations that will result are similar in degree and kind to those told in the fabled stories of such leaders as Abraham Lincoln, Martin Luther King Jr., Mother Teresa, Nelson Mandela, and others. These transformations are also recounted in the simple stories of making a difference, beginning with the first steps, and the risks that each of us take when we stand up for a cause greater than ourselves. Start at a place where you can reasonably determine that you will be effective—think big and bold for a better future, constantly check your purposes and those of others on whom you rely, regenerate ideas and resources to continue your progress, and cherish the opportunity to be a constant student of leadership and your own experience.

6

Leadership Program Design and Continuous Improvement

Designing a purposeful, comprehensive, and useful leadership program for a college or university may seem like a daunting task, especially if the purpose is to provide opportunities that stimulate students to look at the more substantial questions of purpose and meaning in their own lives. However, this task encompasses challenges and possibilities similar to those encountered in many other forms of systemic change.

Many change processes—career and lifestyle decision making, relationship development, and talent development—can be compared to water erosion. The trickle of water begins, cutting the initial crevasse. As the crevasse deepens into a trench, it provides the opportunity for more water to flow through the same channel. Trenches become ditches, which become streams, which combine to become rivers. A study of leadership programs that have emerged and been sustained throughout the nation shows that they had modest beginnings that deepened over time; this flow of purpose allowed those coordinating or working in the program to achieve goals they never thought possible. Those programs that have matured to a sustainable level may now be in a position to cut new and even deeper channels. The complacency that can follow hard work may result in the stagnation of substantial work, and therefore even mature programs require renewal. The insights provided here and the examples to follow in Chapter Seven may open doors you never considered and may lead you to unexpected paths that will eventually take you to places you never imagined.

This chapter proposes that the only way to fully develop the leadership capacity in others is by deliberately crossing a number of boundaries that were assumed to be inviolable. These boundaries may include intellectual assumptions, conflicting research and theoretical evidence, or organizational configurations. Some of the original ideas published in *Student Leadership Programs in Higher Education* (Roberts, 1981) will be recounted as a way of exploring these boundaries. Summaries of the Standards for Student Leadership Programs developed by the Council for the Advancement of Standards (CAS, 1996) and other models will be proposed as frameworks to design or refine boundary-crossing leadership learning opportunities. I will introduce a process model for planning comprehensive leadership programs that take into account the new knowledge bases and experiences that have emerged over the past thirty years, and I will conclude with assessment methods that will infuse continuous improvement into ongoing programs.

Frameworks for Student Leadership Programs

The Leadership Development Task Force of ACPA, the College Student Educators International, first convened in the spring of 1976, following a meeting where student activities workers realized that many campuses were beginning to do more to address leadership issues. The task force worked over the next several years to collect materials from a broad spectrum of campuses that had begun these efforts. The task force then sorted and analyzed the materials and, after numerous meetings and retreats, drafted a set of potential recommendations to present to student affairs staff who wanted to enhance their focus on leadership. The result of this analysis and integration was the publication of *Student Leadership Programs in Higher Education* (Roberts, 1981), which proposed that campuses needed not only to compare notes on what they were doing in leadership but also to seek to develop comprehensive programs that could bring coherence and focus to the quest to enhance students' leadership capabilities. Although the recommendation that leadership programs attend to multiple purposes (training, education, and development) was adopted most widely, attention to multiple strategies and populations was also advocated.

Multiple Purposes, Strategies, and Populations

As the early work in student affairs leadership programs emerged, there were numerous initiatives that worked in their own contexts, having been designed in response to specific needs. The problem was that there wasn't a way to think about what should or should not be included from one campus to another. The resulting analyses further indicated a broad framework of multiple purposes, strategies, and populations, each of which was important in itself.

Multiple Purposes

The framework of training, education, and development was adapted from the work of Leonard Nadler (1970) and proposed three categories that could serve as an umbrella for the types of experiences that leadership program participants might need to have. Training activities included learning activities concretely focused to help the trainee translate a newly acquired insight or skill to an immediate, real situation. Examples that might reflect a training intent are briefings about college or university resources and processes or online modules that teach students how to prepare budget proposals or submit legislation recommending change. Education activities provide "generalizable theories, principles and approaches" that are applicable now and are relevant for future circumstances (p. 20). Examples of leadership education might be briefings on parliamentary procedure, planning and goal-setting processes, or leadership and group dynamic models. Leadership development allows participants "to develop maturity and accompanying insight within the individual" that has a cumulative effect and is based on the cultivation of personal awareness over a longer period of time (p. 20). Examples of leadership development would be intensive living groups, in-depth retreats, personal development courses or series, and programs that incorporate a coach or mentor in guiding participants through these experiences. A detailed developmental model integrating the Perry scheme (Perry, 1998) with the research available on leadership up to 1981 was provided as the last chapter of *Student Leadership Programs in Higher Education*.

Multiple Strategies

Multiple strategies could include an ever-expanding array of pedagogical models, including courses, workshops, retreats, online modules, leadership transcripts, institutes, internships, service-learning, community-based research, and study abroad. In this way, a comprehensive program should provide a number of access points to understanding leadership and should accommodate different student learning styles. One of the challenges in quantifying the outcomes of comprehensive leadership programs is figuring out how to document students' involvement in the various opportunities that are offered. Some campuses have begun to use certificate programs or digital portfolios to help students plan and reflect on their cumulative learning, an idea we will explore later in this chapter.

Multiple Populations

Multiple populations of students need access to leadership learning opportunities. Even in the early days of student affairs programs in leadership, there was a clear recognition that the door needed to be open for any and all students to participate. Numerous programs available on many campuses require applications, selection, or even election. However, the recommendation from beginning to end is that all students deserve access to leadership opportunities in one form or another. Populations that may need focused attention include students of color, women, international, gay, lesbian, bisexual, transgender, and any other students who by virtue of systemic prejudice have not had access and opportunity to exercise leadership from positions of authority. There are other types of student groups and roles within them that may require a different kind of focused attention, such as resident assistants, leaders of fraternal organizations, or students engaged in social change initiatives. Addressing multiple populations ensures that all students recognize their potential to explore and to advance their leadership understanding and capacity.

Standards for Student Leadership Programs

CAS approved its Standards for Student Leadership Programs in 1996. These standards are only one of a broader set of standards available to enhance the effectiveness of programs in residence halls, student activities, counseling, and other areas in student affairs. Based on the same model as these programs, the student leadership program standard focuses on mission; program; leadership; organization and management; human resources; financial resources; facilities, technology, and equipment; legal responsibilities, equal opportunity, access, and affirmative action; campus and community relations; diversity; ethics; and assessment and evaluation. The program description suggested in the CAS Student Leadership Programs standard incorporated much of what was recommended in *Student Leadership Programs in Higher Education* (Roberts, 1981), most notably leadership training, education, and development. Although some campuses have used the standard as the template for self-study and accreditation, there is no accrediting body for leadership programs, nor is any anticipated in the foreseeable future. The International Leadership Association (ILA) initiated a study of its members' preferences about guidelines in 2005; it is possible that ILA will attempt to create guidelines that could complement those of CAS in the future. The CAS standards continue to evolve. Workbooks have been designed to assist campuses in using the standards, and learning outcomes are now available to help programs in setting goals, designing, and assessing the effectiveness of programs. When drafting their learning outcomes statements, designers must exercise great caution to avoid incorporating positional leader assumptions, trait approaches, and other biases that can undermine inclusive leadership.

Leadership in the Making

Kathleen Zimmerman-Oster and John Burkhardt (1999) proposed a number of conditions and strategies that would improve the likelihood of success in leadership programs. These recommendations came out of a series of thirty-one grants the Kellogg Foundation provided from 1990 to 1998 to establish leadership programs on a variety of campuses across the nation. The hallmarks of these programs included recommendations for the context, philosophy, sustainability, and common practice in these programs. The evaluation of the Kellogg Foundation–sponsored grant programs confirmed the comprehensive model proposed in the CAS Student Leadership Programs standard as well as raised additional points related to academic elements and achieving sustainability.

Context

Successful programs are carefully positioned in the context of their particular campus, meaning that there should be a direct and explicit connection between the institutional mission and that of the leadership program. In addition, the program should have broad institutional support, including curricular elements and extracurricular or cocurricular opportunities. The academic portion of the program should transcend any individual department and should ideally include both academic and student affairs staff. Finally, strong leadership by a qualified student affairs professional or faculty member is a key element that ensures credibility.

Philosophy

The Kellogg grant experience indicated that successful programs have a common core intellectual framework. Included among the core ideas is the belief that leadership can and should be developed among young adults. Those leading the program should have explicit theoretical frameworks, should know the literature, and should examine their core values and assumptions in sponsoring the program. There should be a working definition of leadership, though this does not have to be a quotable definition adopted from others' research and theories. Finally, there should be a comprehensive, coordinated approach that includes conventional learning as well as experiential activities, allowing participants to acquire skills while deepening their self-awareness and their leadership knowledge.

Sustainability

One of the most important discoveries of the Kellogg projects was the importance of working toward sustainability. The first variable found to be most important in ensuring the future viability of leadership programs was continuing involvement of a broad spectrum of faculty and administration. Assessment and evaluation are also essential to sustainability; learning outcomes, objectives, and ways to measure progress must be included as strategies for continuous improvement. The leadership program should have a vision and ways to demonstrate that it contributes to the enhancement of the institution.

Common Practices

The Kellogg grant institutions discovered a number of common practices that enhanced the impact and sustainability of these programs. These include self-assessment and reflection; skill building; problem solving; intercultural issues; service-learning and servant leadership; outdoor activities; student leadership of programs; mentoring; community involvement; public policy; targeted training and development; faculty incentives; student recognition; cocurricular transcripts and portfolio development; and capstone experiences. Although this is a long list, a comprehensive program will at least incorporate the ultimate purposes of the initiatives listed earlier. Four ultimate purposes that might be gleaned from this list include self-awareness, testing theory in practice, guidance and coaching, and documentation of outcomes.

The Kellogg grants of the 1990s helped the participating campuses learn many important lessons. The evaluation of the programs confirmed many of the ideas proposed in *Student Leadership Programs in Higher Education* and the CAS Student Leadership Programs standards.

Thinking Integrally

Integral theory (Wilber, 2000) was introduced in Chapter Five to demonstrate progressive stages of consciousness that are relevant to deeper leadership. In addition, integral theory is relevant as a way of conceptualizing the needs of participants in leadership learning opportunities. One of the core ideas of integral theory is the four-quadrant model. This model is the result of crossing two axes: the interior-exterior and the individual-collective. On the interior-exterior axis, the focus is on

Exhibit 6.1: Integral Theory

	INTERIOR	EXTERIOR
INDIVIDUAL	Intentional I—inside the individual (individual development, psychology) Body to Mind to Spirit	Behavioral It—outside of the individual (physical world, physics, chemistry, geology) Gross to Subtle to Causal
COLLECTIVE	Cultural We—inside the collective (interpersonal, and relational) Egocentric (me) to Ethnocentric (us) to Worldcentric (all of us)	Social Its—outside the collective (sociology, anthropology) Group (simple) to Nation (complex) to Global

Note: From *A Theory of Everything,* by K. Wilber, 2000. Boston: Shambhala. Copyright 2000. Reprinted by arrangement with Shambhala Publications, Inc. Boston, MA, www.shambhala.com.

whether the consideration is inside or outside the participant. On the individual-collective axis, the focus is on the participant or on the collective, community level. Crossing the two axes proposes that there are four areas on which to concentrate when exploring an integral perspective: I, it, we, and its.

The "I" quadrant (Intentional) reflects the internal world of our subjective experience. It includes the degree to which we have developed an identity, and it embraces physical, intellectual, and faith awareness. This progression is from body to mind to spirit. Attention to this quadrant is like laying a cornerstone. If individuals have not explored their own interior spaces to determine their values and purposes in life, progressing in leadership will be a challenge.

The "it" quadrant (Behavioral) is the objective world outside of ourselves, but it is still about how we individually relate to the world, manifested in our behavior. This progression is from gross to subtle to causal. These three levels reflect the degree of consciousness we have of the world. The gross body state reflects simply being awake and aware of physical surroundings. The subtle state involves dreaming and imagining. The causal state is related to deep dreaming and the profound awareness that can come from it. Using "it" to characterize this quadrant reflects more of the object awareness that comes from gross body consciousness; the other two move us beyond the physical realm.

The "we" quadrant (Cultural) is subjective but related to collective experiences with others. This collective is the culture in which we live, whether that culture is a small group of close associates or family or whether it is a community of practice, such as a learning or working group. This progression is from egocentric to ethnocentric to worldcentric views. Egocentric views are focused on individual welfare. Ethnocentric views are related to the affiliation group. Worldcentric views move to a level of understanding the interconnectedness of the many groups and systems in our world.

The "its" quadrant (Social) is outside the individual and collective, extending to the social systems and the physical environment in which we live. The developmental progression includes increasingly expanding circles of association from groups that allow us to survive all the way to environmental systems that enhance life and allow for the advancement of the human condition. This progression is from group to nation to global.

The combination of issues involved in integral theory's four-quadrant model allows those designing leadership learning opportunities to broaden the conceptual framework of their focus, thereby articulating the various levels of impact that might result. There are examples where other models or programs have already addressed the four quadrants. For example, the Social Change Model of Leadership Development (Astin & Astin, 2000) clusters the 7 C's into a model moving from the individual to the group to society at large. These three levels are consonant with the "I," "we," and "its" quadrants of integral theory, and even the "it" quadrant could be seen as the way behavior (it) is expressed in groups and in actions focused on social change.

Integral theory and its four-quadrant strategy can be used as a theoretical model to help students understand the interrelatedness of individual, group, societal, and environmental implications of their behavior. Such a perspective could be used as a lens to test whether there are stakeholders whose perspectives are not being considered in a leadership action. Or integral theory could be used to analyze the degree of attention placed on individual, group, and collective dynamics in a comprehensive leadership program.

The critical aspect of an integral perspective is that the four quadrants impact each other, and the presumption is that progress in any one quadrant is limited or enhanced by progress in the others. In addition, each quadrant represents potentially greater complexity through its three developmental stages or levels, such as from body to mind to spirit. The degree of detail one needs to understand the progression will influence the choice of a theoretical model among the many theoretical models that have been proposed by those who have researched elements of the four quadrants.

In the "I" quadrant, Perry (1998), Kegan (1994), Gilligan (1982), Fowler (1981), and others might be used as the theoretical framework to allow for the identification of greater detail as individuals move from one stage of complexity to another as one example.

The other proposal of integral theory is that there are broad differences in the developmental complexity in the four quadrants. There are those around us who are relatively inexperienced and undeveloped, and others who are highly complex and advanced in their perspectives. Integral theory honors all the levels of development and advocates that each is adequate and appropriate for its own circumstance. When people recognize and honor the variation, greater opportunity emerges to interconnect everyone's experiences and perspectives, thus benefiting all those involved.

Choosing a Framework

Multiple purposes, strategies, and populations. Self-designed and directed leadership portfolios. Majors, minors, or certificates—and others. All of these are possible pieces of a framework that might make sense to students as well as guide those who design and deliver the leadership learning initiatives on a particular campus. The critical question is how to decide on the framework that will be most useful in your setting. As might be expected, the answer to that is, "It depends." The key to designing and redesigning leadership programs is that it has to be done in the context of the campus and in full consideration of the major stakeholders whose involvement is essential to ensure the initiative's success. The next section provides steps and recommendations for a process that would be sensitive to the institutional context while exploring a breadth of program options.

Expanding Framework for Leadership Learning

The Kellogg Foundation study and recommendations completed by Zimmerman-Oster and Burkhardt (1999) concluded that leadership programs must be broadly conceived and aligned with the vision and goals of the institution in order to be most effective. This necessitates that they be purposefully related to the academic mission. The original *Student Leadership Programs in Higher Education* (Roberts, 1981) comprehensive model was conceived to be essentially extracurricular or cocurricular, or both. Extracurricular activities refer to those exclusively provided outside of class and not for credit. Cocurricular activities are those having a relationship to coursework, but not the coursework itself. Examples of cocurricular activities are service-learning for which students receive no grade, attending lectures or concerts that extend learning beyond the classroom, or independent work done for no credit. Although the distinctions may seem slight, there is a real difference in how faculty generally perceive these terms. Student affairs staffs have long been involved in extracurricular and cocurricular events, and there are numerous examples in leadership where they also teach, but their primary role is not in the classroom.

It is interesting in itself that the Leadership Development Task Force of the 1970s addressed little of what was happening through classroom instruction. Perhaps this was because the idea of leadership programs was so new that there wasn't much available in the curriculum. Or the mental models of learning that constrained the task force may have kept them from recognizing initiatives that were already under way through full-time faculty teaching in the curriculum. Whatever the reason, the emerging and current realization among many student affairs staff is that, although useful, extracurricular and cocurricular programs cannot have their intended impact without reaching more broadly across the campus to others in academic affairs and beyond.

As I proposed in Chapter Two, perhaps it is time to declare new language to reflect the joint roles played by faculty and student affairs staff in studying and cultivating leadership. The models we use and the processes we undertake must be different, broader, and clearly more inclusive; advocacy for leadership learning seems like the kind of approach that will embrace contributions from all the stakeholders. Leadership learning needs to draw from all relevant theories and models, invite others to the table, and test and build the program as it is progressively implemented. The following processes and principles provide suggestions for how to do this; they are adapted from an article first published in *Building Leadership Bridges* (Roberts, 2003).

Planning Recommendations

The question of how to construct leadership experiences and learning that acknowledges the changing world around us is raised frequently on practically every listserv of which I'm a part and in most conference programs on leadership. It is interesting that in the digital world there are so many individuals eager to jump in to answer the question when it is raised. The generative inclination of colleagues who are engaged in these listserv exchanges provide considerable useful advice. However, there are almost always considerations that are not mentioned or that are left unexamined.

Having helped design four leadership programs on different campuses as well as having talked with many colleagues over the years about the critical steps to take in designing or redesigning leadership programs, I have found that there are several issues to consider and a deliberate process to undertake that will enhance success in the design or redesign and renewal process.

Issues to Consider Before You Begin

The following are ideas to consider before you begin the process of designing initiatives to advance leadership learning:

- Change the purpose of leadership programs away from leader development focused on individuals (Rost, 1991, 1993) to helping all students develop their skills and capacities in leadership.

- Make as many leadership development opportunities available to all students as is possible. Where resource implications restrain this intent, make a commitment to begin with pilot efforts that will intentionally expand over time.

- Critically examine every act, message, speaker, and process to tease out the lessons the institution explicitly and implicitly conveys about leadership. Foster a campus culture that reflects what you espouse about learning and shared leadership. Shaping culture entails persistent effort over an extended period and includes everything from rituals and traditions to the way students, faculty, and staff are included or excluded in decision making.

Background Preparation and Perspective

Once these ideas have been considered and preliminary determinations made, planning should proceed in a sequence roughly equivalent to the following preparatory steps:

1. Study your college or university mission statement to determine what it espouses about leadership, civic engagement, service, and other related priorities.
2. Advocate for a broad cross-section of faculty and staff to share in the responsibility of developing leadership capacity in students.
3. Seek the input of institutional decision makers and change agents—positional and nonpositional.

The Comprehensive Planning Process

Once the preparatory steps are completed, designing or revising leadership learning opportunities should proceed with the following progressive steps:

1. Convene a planning group composed of individuals who have demonstrated an ability to think "outside the box" and who appear willing to work together on the project. Foster a sense of mutual exploration of what is in the institution's best interest and what the members of the group seek to accomplish.

2. If your planning group is redesigning or renewing the campus leadership learning model, take time to reflect on what has been accomplished and the areas for greatest potential improvement.

3. Conduct a survey of the literature that the planning group perceives as critical to a cutting-edge perspective on leadership. Incorporate multiple disciplinary perspectives, experiential methods, and new pedagogies that will ensure innovation in your design or redesign.

4. Agree to common language about how the planning group defines "leading" and "leadership." Differentiate these terms and include the implications of each term on the perceptions of potential participants.

5. Gather information about the nature of the campus culture and the attitudes and values of students. If longitudinal information is available, determine trends that have been sustained or are changing.

6. Relate what you seek as change agents in learning to what you know of leadership, the institutional mission, and the nature of your students.

7. Begin the design or redesign process for a comprehensive leadership program that develops the capacity for leadership in all students. Consider also the coincidental implications for faculty and staff leadership learning.

8. Consider the CAS Standards for Student Leadership Programs as a broad template to help identify the core ideas, organization, resources, and other variables that affect success.

9. Gather information through benchmarking or consultant advice to enhance the quality and focus of the program design.

10. Keep your ideas provisional and flexible and seek community input.

11. Solicit suggestions for revision of the provisional model while inviting various constituents to become partners in developing leadership potential in students.

12. Conduct baseline assessment of students' educational attainment; gather and compile information that already exists.

13. Look at input from "partners" to see how a purposeful and coherent comprehensive program can be constructed.

14. Create a staffing model that includes faculty, student affairs, and other staff. Use unconventional clusters and relationship networks to enhance the breadth of participants while also identifying champions for leadership learning who will help guide the continuing collaborative work.

15. Consider carefully the implications for potential campus culture changes. Culture can serve as either a powerful contradiction or reinforcement for the leadership learning you seek to achieve.

16. Acquire the resources required to begin implementation. Do not attempt to fully fund everything the planning group wishes to do. Acquire enough resources to get started and then rigorously evaluate and promote what is accomplished as you go.

Pilot and Progressive Initiatives

Once the model for leadership learning is determined, ambitious yet modest aspiration is key. It will take time for broad leadership learning to take hold, and new initiatives are best viewed as pilot efforts that will be evaluated and redesigned for constant improvement. In addition, these strategies will help continue to build support for the emerging or refined program:

- If your planning process is focused on renewal of an existing program, determine the implications for preexisting initiatives and make sure that staff from any program already in place are invited to join in positive enhancement.

- Build bridges by acting as catalysts and orchestrators—invite all those who are stakeholders or anyone who can contribute through whatever means to join in the effort to deepen leadership. In spirit, give the program away at every opportunity.

- Develop an identity for what you advocate and offer—relate to others in ways that are inclusive and help others see their aspirations in your initiative.

- Constantly reassess progress, redesign, and initiate new aspects of the comprehensive program so that it becomes more pervasive and inclusive.

- Celebrate your accomplishment in establishing a leadership learning model that fosters connections and will be constantly renewed and renewing for the campus community.

The aforementioned issues, background preparation, and planning steps include attention to the assumptions behind our work, in-depth analysis of the campus environment, and listening to the many stakeholder groups that could benefit from and will want to contribute to such an important initiative. It is important not to neglect any of those whom you will want to serve as advocates. In cases where the planning process is directed toward the redesign or renewal of an existing program, constantly reinforce that the work previously done was not incorrect or flawed in any way. Circumstances, times, and available resources change and any cutting-edge program requires ongoing renewal in order to achieve its aims.

Steady and Persistent

The metaphor that introduced this chapter can be used as a reminder of how long and hard the work of planning and implementing leadership programs can be. The gradual channeling necessary for a stream to turn into a river can take a very long time. The metaphor also conveys the importance of taking the welcoming course. It is not unusual for programs to run into resistance. Like water, the most effective program design strategy may be to direct the energy around the target rather than right into it. Water has a mighty force once smaller streams begin to coalesce into a larger body, such as a river. So it is with leadership learning. Once there is momentum behind the program, it takes on a life of its own and it is important to stand back and let others get involved and earn credit for their contributions.

Assessment and using it to stimulate continuous improvement is another force that can be used to constantly challenge and channel the advancements of an individual leadership initiative or a broader comprehensive program.

Assessment to Renew Leadership Learning

Although this chapter is titled "Leadership Program Design and Continuous Improvement," I am including a section on assessment, because assessment is integral to an ongoing commitment to improve effectiveness. I will introduce leadership assessment with brief framing comments. I will then describe the emerging work of the Multi-Institution Study of Leadership Development (Komives & Dugan, 2006), and I will introduce a rubric for assessment proposed by a team of leadership educators in collaboration with the StudentVoice organization.

Challenges and Opportunities of Assessing Leadership Learning in Students

Assessment of higher education outcomes has been becoming more of a priority for a number of years. How state and federal mandates will unfold in the future is unclear. Regardless of the external pressures to assess the impact of all educational opportunity, most educators believe that assessment is key to understanding student progress, which then contributes to refining and enhancing programs.

As we seek to understand students' progress in learning about leadership, it is important to keep in mind the concerns that assessment experts pose. For instance, Trudy Banta (2006) warns against adopting standardized instruments that claim to measure achievement in learning. Such instruments, she says, may be particularly ineffective in measuring value-added gains because they do not provide control for pre-existing differences among students (Banta & Pike, 2007). Standardized measures also fail because of the tests' generic questions, which may lead to inconclusive evidence or may fall short in their ability to compare groups of students on one campus and, especially, to compare student achievement across different institutional settings.

Banta and Pike (2007) recommend that assessment in collegiate settings focus on measures of content mastery in academic majors coupled with electronic portfolios and workforce readiness measures. If such a strategy were to be undertaken in leadership learning, leadership studies faculty would need to agree on the content they believe is central to understanding the dynamics and nuances of leading and leadership. Faculty and student affairs staff would then need to determine the degree to which experiences inside and outside of class would be reflected in the documentation that students could submit in electronic portfolios. Both faculty and staff would need to engage with employers of college graduates to determine the workplace insights, skills, and capacities that would be desirable in employees, and then begin to measure progress toward fostering such qualities among students. Banta (2006) posits that the student portfolio is the most authentic and comprehensive assessment of general student learning. To fulfill the potential of portfolio learning and assessment, faculty and staff would need to create rubrics to assess learning outcomes across a variety of experiences, technology enhancements would be required to allow for sophisticated creation and compilation of portfolios, and students would need to enter artifacts into their portfolios throughout their undergraduate years. Finally, students, faculty, and staff would have to be serious about completing and assessing progress through portfolio review. These are challenging conditions, but they may very well be more desirable than standing on the sidelines while standardized instruments are created to assess the work of leadership learning in ways that will be inadequate for us all.

In addition to the broad concerns and implications of various assessment methods, there are other specific issues related to measuring leadership learning. One of the major challenges we face in assessing the impact of leadership learning is that our assessments are frequently only of the self-selected students who participate in our courses and programs. The second challenge is that most of these assessments are heavily tipped in the direction of measuring satisfaction rather than progress toward learning goals, or they collect self-reports of students' progress. Although satisfaction and self-reporting are helpful, they have limited usefulness in identifying potential areas of improvement, especially when the focus is on learning or developmental outcomes.

Hannum, Martineau, and Reinelt (2006) provide a comprehensive overview and examples of evaluation in leadership programs in for-profit, not-for-profit, community, and other settings. The various chapters in this edited volume include numerous examples from the work of the Center for Creative Leadership. With a focus on evaluation that is fair and stimulates an ongoing commitment to learning, there are many ideas that could be adapted for use in higher education leadership learning. Two specific ideas that hold great promise are looking more intentionally at return on investment and evaluating the link between leadership development and organizational performance. Delving into these areas could enhance the credibility of leadership programs immeasurably. Although those in education are not accustomed to looking at ideas such as return on investment, Phillips and Phillips (2006) provide a conceptual framework that could allow evaluators to compare the number of students involved, degree of impact, and related costs of various kinds of programs. Analyses of this type would be extremely helpful in situations where resources are limited or when progressive implementation of new initiatives is the only feasible way to proceed. LeMay and Ellis (2006) provide additional important guidance on how leadership learning could be evaluated in relation to the impact on the broader organization. Examples of improving organizational effectiveness might include the level of understanding members have of the purpose and direction of the organization, the degree to which organizational resources are allocated in line with the organization's strategic direction, or that the organization is recognized for its commitment to continuous learning, and members demonstrate a continued willingness to innovate, even in the face of setbacks. Return on investment and the impact of leadership learning on organizational effectiveness are just two of many ideas that could be extrapolated, modified, and applied in higher education to stimulate the constant improvement of our work.

As leadership learning becomes a greater institutional focus, outcomes in leadership learning should be documented among the general student population, among students who take courses or participate in programs of leadership learning, and among students who are involved in a variety of leadership capacities ranging from student government officers to the grassroots informal leadership of social change groups.

There are many other issues that influence assessment of leadership learning, but with these cautions as context, I turn to two examples of leadership assessment that, if carefully launched, could provide critical information about our successes and greater opportunities.

Multi-Institution Study of Leadership

Although the Multi-Institution Study of Leadership (Komives & Dugan, 2006) was conceived as a limited assessment study, the response to the targeted invitation to institutions resulted in an overwhelming fifty-two participating institutions and over sixty thousand respondents. The implications of this study are only beginning to unfold, and it is very likely that studies spinning out of the original measure and follow-up studies over the years will begin to dominate much of the literature in leadership assessment. The Multi-Institution Study of Leadership (MSL) was implemented as a web-based survey and included a scale to measure the Social Change Model of Leadership Development noted in Chapter Three as well as other scales or questions related to cognitive development, diversity appreciation, activism, leadership identity, and leadership efficacy. Specifically related to the shortcomings of many leadership assessments, the MSL was administered to random samples of students and allowed for control of preprogram experiences and comparison of students based on the kinds of experiences they had in leadership learning.

The general findings of the MSL are of great interest, as are the specific institutional analyses that each of the fifty-two participating institutions are beginning to pursue. The MSL findings reflect that college students are generally confident in their leadership abilities and that these abilities progress from first-year to graduation in all of the Social Change model capacities. The greatest growth as students matured was in "consciousness of self" and the two areas of least change were "controversy with civility" and "change." "Commitment" was the capacity students rated the highest overall.

Men and women differed in their measurements of confidence in leadership, with men reporting higher confidence than women. However, women reported higher levels than men on all the Social Change model scales. Students who reported being from marginalized groups reported the highest levels of comfort with change. Students with far-right or conservative political orientations reported greater self-confidence in leadership than those who reported being far left or liberal. Previous research about the value of students' collegiate experiences was confirmed in leadership learning; those who were involved with at least one activity on campus reported higher leadership capacities on all scales. This effect was more exaggerated when the depth of involvement increased. Opportunity to partake in leadership training or education was also related to increases in positive reports on the Social Change model scales. Repeated short- and medium-term experiences, coupled with the opportunity to engage in leadership, resulted in the most pronounced changes. The final MSL variable I will note here is that students who had experience with faculty, student affairs staff, employer, community member, or other student mentors reported greater leadership confidence, and the more mentor-protégé experiences they had, the higher the confidence.

As a way of demonstrating how particular campuses might use the MSL data to understand their own environments, Miami University analyzed students' experiences with mentors to see if students had less, the same, or greater access to this potentially powerful aspect of undergraduate education. The data indicated that Miami students reported slightly higher levels of access to mentors across all groups except employers and community members. Even though there are far fewer student affairs staff in comparison to the total number of faculty, staff, students, and community members available to serve as mentors, student affairs staff were well represented among the number of initial mentor contacts. Faculty and students served as the most frequent mentors at the middle levels of contact, and students served most frequently at the highest levels of contact. Attempting to interpret these data for enhancement, one might conclude that the greatest potential gain in influencing students' experiences in leadership would be through designing faculty and peer-to-peer mentor relationships that are more purposeful and frequent. Whether these findings would be applicable in other settings would have to be explored on a campus-by-campus basis. If the same pattern did exist, it would be extremely helpful to know that faculty and students needed to be leveraged more effectively in students' mentor-protégé experiences in order to deepen the impact of leadership learning. This is only one small example that could be drawn from the MSL study. There are many, many more possibilities.

In the MSL example, Banta and Pike's cautions are at least partially addressed. The study involved a random sample of students so that the analysis of the data included studying the experiences of all types of students and across all levels of campus engagement. Although the MSL is a standardized instrument, it is not an achievement measurement, the type about which Banta expressed most concern. The MSL has coherence as an instrument because it is based on a specific model and includes additional scales related to other specific research questions. The MSL includes precondition indicators that allow researchers to analyze the results based on cultural or experiential differences, and it also allows for comparison among various subgroups that exist on most campuses. The qualitative assessment advocated by Banta is not possible with a broad study such as the MSL. However, as the following description of the leadership program rubric indicates, the MSL could easily be part of a broader array of assessment strategies that might include portfolios, tracking, and other approaches.

A Multimeasure Rubric to Assess Leadership Learning

Curt Brungardt and Chris Crawford (1996) proposed a model of leadership assessment that was adapted, used in conference presentations, and served as the stimulus in designing a leadership assessment rubric with StudentVoice. This model advises that progress in acquiring leadership insights, knowledge, and capacities should include multiple types of information, including tracking of participation, reactions of participants, knowledge and learning, leadership self-awareness, corollary impact, and behavior. Each of these information sources provides a different angle on leadership learning outcomes, and together they help us move beyond satisfaction and self-report.

Tracking

When leadership learning becomes a pervasive part of a campus environment, keeping track of who participates and to what degree becomes a challenge. However, this information becomes very powerful when linked to learning outcomes, corollary impacts, and other categories. Campus information technology systems such as SCTBanner now provide the possibility to link these previously disconnected sources of information. One example is that students' educational attainment (their grades and retention) could be correlated with the degree to which they participate in leadership learning and experiences. In another example, patterns of student participation could be analyzed to determine if different subpopulations participate at the same or different levels.

Reactions

This is perhaps the easiest information to gather and includes satisfaction, the degree to which students found the ideas helpful, and suggestions on additional issues where students need help. These data can lead to useful recommendations for program improvement and identification of unmet leadership learning needs.

Knowledge and Learning

There are vast sources of knowledge about leadership from multiple disciplines and perspectives. The recall, integration, and application of this knowledge places helpful lenses in the hands and hearts of students of leadership. Acquisition of knowledge related to specific theories, models, processes, and skills is precisely what Banta and Pike (2007) recommended as the most defensible and rational content-based assessment strategy.

Leadership Self-Awareness

The presence, flow, and oscillation deeper leadership model requires a greater depth of personal awareness than is typical of many learning areas. Therefore, determining the degree to which students have developed a deeper and more realistic awareness of themselves is of central importance. Students should know more about their personal strengths and vulnerabilities and about their personality and how it is perceived by others. In addition, they should have a way of understanding their relative proficiencies so that they can judge their need for further learning.

Corollary Impact

This is information compiled about students, which includes data about students' impact on the institution or community, increased opportunities for involvement and service, independent research accomplishments, number of fellowships and awards students receive, and other campus-based recognition.

Behavior

Behavior indicators might come from students' self-reports. However, other measures of behavior might include advisers' reports, member and participant perceptions, or observations. To control for self-selection effects, behavioral measures would likely be more effective if they were taken before and after students' participation in specific leadership learning experiences, or these could be incorporated as a before and after measure in a four-year portfolio. Important behaviors to include are congruence of thought and action, taking responsibility, genuineness and mutuality of relationships, and ethical decision making.

These six areas, and perhaps others deemed important by the campus as it designs its assessment model, could be combined with measures related to participants, all students, organizational effectiveness, and the campus or community environment.

Exhibit 6.2: Assessment

	PARTICI- PANTS	ALL STUDENTS	ORGANIZA- TION EFFEC- TIVENESS	CAMPUS/ COMMUNITY
TRACKING				
REACTION				
KNOWLEDGE AND LEARNING				
LEADERSHIP SELF- AWARENESS				
COROLLARY IMPACT				
BEHAVIOR				

Combining these into a matrix like that shown in Exhibit 6.2 would allow planners to determine assessment collection methods and areas to target for change, thus helping them focus on the outcomes of leadership learning at multiple levels.

When considering how to collect the assessment information, multiple strategies may be needed. When change over time among students at large is assessed, a cohort model may be useful. The cohort model could identify subgroups of students who would participate in annual assessments to help determine what changes occur over time. Pre- and postmeasures of the overall student population or of specific program participants could provide a more direct measure of change linked to involvement in leadership learning. One-time cross-sectional studies could be employed in other models, leading to a determination of how full participants in leadership learning differ from those who are marginally or minimally engaged.

Use of the leadership assessment rubric can help institutions avoid the critique offered by Banta and others. Specifically, the very student portfolio that Banta (2006) advocates as the most authentic, comprehensive, and useful could become the repository of the rubric evidence noted here: tracking, reactions, knowledge, self-awareness, corollary impact, and behavior. These could all be compiled into a comprehensive portfolio review that would be both a learning tool and documentation of the powerful outcome of these leadership learning experiences.

Assessing Leadership Learning Programs

In addition to assessing the leadership learning among participants and students at large, the program itself may benefit from assessment. Every campus that is accredited undergoes a cycle of ten-year self-study preparation for the visits of accreditation committees. Leadership learning of a variety of types should be included in these reviews. Assessment is an ideal opportunity to gain visibility for the efforts of those coordinating these activities and helps relate leadership learning to outcomes that are a priority throughout the institution. Roberts and Ullom (1989) suggested that the needs of a broad range of constituents should be assessed as leadership learning is enhanced and that the important proof of the outcome is whether or not these same stakeholders report positive gain after implementation of new initiatives. Because of the marginalization that such groups frequently experience, it would be particularly important to consider the needs of specific populations, including women; students of color; international students; students with disabilities; and gay, lesbian, bisexual, and transgender students.

A commitment to assessing leadership learning resulting from coursework introduces additional special concerns. This is an area in which initial conversations have just begun within the International Leadership Association. If guidelines are established, they could be used for leadership studies programs such as majors, minors, concentrations, and certificates. The initial reaction has been cautious, primarily out of fear that prescriptive accreditation may follow the creation of guidelines. However, many believe that the credibility of the curricular approaches to leadership are dependent on establishing standards and greater rigor in all programs. Particularly because of the potential creation of guidelines, leadership studies programs will be incorporated into self-studies and accreditation reviews in the future. As this occurs, leadership educators coming from faculty and student affairs alike have the opportunity to demonstrate the critical interplay and cooperation between curricular and cocurricular life that has been advocated in this book.

Enhancing Attention to Assessment

Few would argue that assessing the impact of leadership learning is unimportant. Formulating assessment methods is best addressed during the design and redesign of any comprehensive program. Internal comparisons across levels of participation over time and use of multiple kinds of assessment data will serve leadership educators well. The purpose of both the StudentVoice project and the MSL was to offer methods that allow benchmark comparisons. Ideally, each of our campuses will be able to compare with other institutions that have related models, similar student populations, or purposes. These benchmarking comparisons should not be done for competitive reasons but with an eye toward sharing best practices to improve everyone's practice. In all of our assessment efforts we should be on guard to control for student characteristics and experiences that can potentially skew the findings of our assessments. Examples include previous participation in churches, synagogues, mosques, and other faith organizations, community organizations, sports, military, and service groups. The bottom line is to design assessment that allows leadership educators to continuously improve and advance the pedagogies, processes, and focus of our programs.

Critical Questions and Guidance in Assessment and Evaluation

Hannum, Martineau, and Reinelt (2006, pp. 560–564) concluded their extensive review of evaluation in leadership programs by posing five important questions that may warrant consideration as the focus on leadership learning continues to evolve in higher education:

> What is the best way to identify and match the "right" individuals, teams, and communities with the "right" leadership development?
>
> How are leadership development outcomes affected when leadership is developed "at home" or "in place"?
>
> What program components are most strongly related to which program outcomes?
>
> What are the stages or pathways for individual and collective leadership development?
>
> What are promising methods for evaluating collective leadership development?
>
> How does culture influence leadership development initiatives and evaluations?

The fact that these questions were universally raised across business, community, service, education, and many other arenas of leadership provides considerable common ground that could allow those of us in higher education to connect more purposefully and powerfully with a broader range of stakeholders.

In addition to the questions just listed, Hannum et al. (2006, p. 565) provide five recommendations for those designing, implementing, and consuming leadership learning evaluations:

> Involve stakeholders at all stages of the process in order to appropriately consider multiple needs and perspectives.
>
> Design the evaluation before the initiative is implemented.
>
> Clarify outcomes to the extent possible with stakeholders, recognizing that there may be different kinds and levels of outcomes.

Discuss the purpose of the evaluation and how information will be used before beginning the evaluation.

Use multiple measures to gather information about complex or vague outcomes from multiple perspectives.

When assessment and evaluation of leadership learning include attention to these commitments, the quality of the assessment and its usefulness and effectiveness in enhancing practice will result in rapid and progressive improvement over time.

Resources and Final Notes

In addition to the models provided through the early research on leadership programs and the subsequent testing completed through the Kellogg Foundation–sponsored programs, there are several other resources that can assist those who wish to create or enhance their leadership programs. Although the Center for Creative Leadership is focused more on business and professional leadership than on student leadership development, it generates and compiles numerous resources that can stimulate new thinking in educational settings. There are professional associations such as the International Leadership Association that draw together those who study and practice leadership in a variety of settings. The ACPA College Educators International and the National Association of Student Personnel Administrators have subgroups that regularly explore leadership questions; these groups frequently bind together and with others to provide conferences or draft publications that are helpful. The National Clearinghouse for Leadership Programs is available through the University of Maryland as an ongoing and critical repository for ideas and models. One of the newest publications available to clearinghouse members is the *Handbook for Student Leadership Programs* (Komives et al., 2006). Finally, of the private foundations committed to advancing leadership learning, the most active are the Kellogg Foundation and the Kettering Foundation.

———————

If we are to be successful in fulfilling the promise of leadership studies and development, we need to find ways to more purpose-fully connect the work of those who study, practice, and develop leadership capacity in students. Advocating for a more inclusive approach to leadership learning has the potential to draw many more partners together in a common search for understanding as we work to develop leadership potential in ourselves and others. The connections and mutual support that we establish are very powerful.

As more programs have become stable, it has become increasingly important to renew and refresh the commitments our institutions have made to leadership learning. In today's com-plex world, evolving leadership research, the implications of such research, and innovations in our institutional environments serve as healthy catalysts for change, and we should welcome these opportunities.

Four essential commitments will enhance the prospect of creat-ing a pervasive and shared commitment to leadership learning. The first of these is to seek to create a campus culture that reflects and reinvigorates the goal of leadership learning. No campus is a perfect reflection of all the things that research has indicated characterize healthy and thriving organizations; don't let your own institutional imperfections hold you back from aspiring to something better. The second commitment that will enhance the impact of leader-ship learning is to share it and to give it away. Leadership most effectively draws others in when positioned as being inclusive, transformative, and adaptive. Others can easily see their needs and interests being served through leadership learning when defined this way. The third commitment is to constantly challenge the mental models of learning and leadership in the campus environment. As we saw in Chapter One, higher education has evolved in ways that may not serve our nation and the globe well in the twenty-first century. As leadership learning advocates more effective mental models and organizational structures, it might become one of the primary stimuli for organizational transformation at those institutions that need it most. The last commitment is a practical implication of the other three. Commitment to innovative models of staffing will guarantee attention and focus as well as shared responsibility for leadership learning among as many stakeholders as possible. Those who champion leadership learning should seek to think and act collaboratively, even when the institutional context seems to reinforce responding to vested interests and political agendas. Challenge your own way of thinking and broaden the investment of all potential advocates and partners.

7

Innovations to Deepen Leadership

The definition of leadership I proposed in Chapter Five was simple: conviction in action. In addition, I proposed that conviction had to be discovered within the context of human experience and with the recognition that all of us are bound together in common striving and fulfillment. In this chapter, I turn to how this kind of conviction might be discovered and nurtured. The discovery of worthy work can unfold through the steps of the Presence model, which include seeing, sensing, presencing, envisioning, enacting, and embodying. In addition, flow encourages one to remain constant to the vision. Finally, oscillation allows one to achieve creativity and high performance. This chapter will explore how presence, flow, and oscillation can be used to formulate a comprehensive approach to leadership learning that includes faculty, student affairs staff, and students in pursuing deeper leadership.

Presence, Flow, and Oscillation in Collegiate Leadership

There are many wonderful and influential leadership learning initiatives throughout higher education. These cover the gamut from speakers, conferences, workshops, retreats, residential programs, service-learning activities, resource centers, peer-led programs, programs for special populations, internships, outdoor experiential learning, institutes, single courses, academic concentrations, minors, majors, and more. This section will not attempt to cover the full range of practice. Other sources of information have been developed (such as the work of Komives et al., 2006) or are constantly being updated in electronic form (such as from the National Clearinghouse for Leadership Programs) that will serve you well in staying abreast of the field. My purpose in this section will be to provide examples of programs that are unusual or that have distinctive offerings within the deeper leadership framework of presence, flow, and oscillation. The examples are out of my own experience or drawn from other campuses; all are examples of leadership learning previously or presently in use.

Presence

The Presence model includes six progressive stages: seeing, sensing, presencing, envisioning, enacting, and embodying. Each stage informs the stage that follows it so that there is a cumulative effect. However, throughout life, one likely explores the stages in the Presence model multiple times. As a simple example, my older daughter, Devin, struggled to identify a career when she was in college. Devin returned for a holiday break in her sophomore year and announced that she did not see any sense in returning to classes the next semester because she did not know what to do with her life. After the initial panic of a father whose offspring was experiencing textbook career moratorium, we discussed that learning is not always focused on a specific objective, but that much of it is intended to cultivate broadly applicable knowledge, insights, and skills that can be used in a variety of endeavors. The conclusion was that Devin took a deep breath, returned to school, continued her part-time job, and pursued the completion of her liberal education requirements. Her part-time job in a local restaurant became something that she deeply enjoyed, and she started thinking about the catering and event management field. She eventually decided that a marketing major followed by a culinary arts certificate would set her up to own her own business someday. She allowed herself to have patience with the career decision-making process, explored options at a surface level, and then deepened her commitment as the path became clearer to her. She followed the presence stages, but she moved through the stages at deeper and deeper levels as she refined her commitment.

Moreover, the Presence model brings to our awareness issues of much greater profundity than just career decisions. Presence is about the eventual discovery of ultimate purposes for being—the true calling of vocation. A conversation between Ken Wilber and Otto Scharmer (2003) indicated that the stages of presence can be observed in most intermediate stages of human development, especially those stages characteristic of most young adults' lives. Wilber related presence to his own notions of integral theory by proposing that presence helps move people through deeper states of consciousness at whatever stage they are in. Even more important, Wilber proposed that repeated plunges into deeper states of consciousness can speed developmental progress, much as some developmental theories note that reflection facilitates growth by helping students process their experiences. The proposal that the stages of presence can be explored at varying developmental levels and that repeated pursuit of them has the potential to accelerate development opens up incredible opportunities in leadership learning.

The leadership learning possibilities that follow are clustered within the six stages of presence, although many of the initiatives could have potential influence in students' experiences in different or perhaps multiple stages of the model. Open mind, open heart, and open will can also serve as other words to reflect the ever-deepening work of leadership—deeper work that takes us to the gut or core of leadership.

Downloading

The first stage in the Presence model is seeing, which is preceded by the initial commitment to explore more critically ("download") one's previous assumptions. To download is to discard previous notions and preconceived ways of thinking that could restrict a fuller exploration of the dynamics of any particular problem or question.

Considering the diversity of perspectives related to leadership that students receive before coming to college, as well as the persistence of public examples that leading is the purview of privileged individuals in positions of power and authority, it is of primary importance to encourage students to carefully examine their previous views of leadership. Critical examination could occur by attending campus lectures, observing speakers at leadership conferences, and participating in introductory courses in leadership, and, at a deeper level, by traveling abroad.

Campus lectures are a readily available resource that can introduce leadership questions. Who speaks and the message they deliver is many times out of our realm of control. However, what is always available to us is a critically reflective conversation about how the speaker was introduced, what the speaker said, and the images evoked by both. It does not really matter if the images are consistent or inconsistent with the view of leadership that campus programs espouse; either way, there is opportunity to critically reflect, compare, and contrast these perspectives. Considering the expense of many speakers these days, it is not only logical but also good educational practice to encourage students to gather together in classrooms, residence halls, or leadership classes to tease out the lessons of leadership from these events.

Many campuses schedule specific speakers as leadership conference keynotes or as stand-alone lectures on leadership. In these cases, those sponsoring the speaker can have greater influence in shaping the message to reinforce or to deliberately critique leadership issues. One of the frustrations with contracted speakers is that many of them have prepared speeches that they routinely deliver. If not asked to do otherwise, they will proceed without consideration for how their ideas reinforce or challenge ideas about leadership that the institution in general or the sponsoring program in particular seeks to communicate. To overcome this challenge, Miami University created a speakers' agreement that communicated a set of values that were important to the campus, such as intellectual rigor, respect for individual difference, and inclusive leadership. When speakers receive their university contract to speak, they are asked to respect the university's commitment to building a positive campus climate and advocating leadership as a shared responsibility of all those in the community. If speakers have contrasting ideas, it then becomes their responsibility to engage in respectful discourse about the differences.

Introductory courses in leadership can drive critical examination to a more substantial level. Consideration of how leadership has been viewed over time by different authors, researchers, and theorists is included in many courses and the texts that are used in them. This kind of introduction helps explain why there are so many different contemporary views of leadership—views that are carried over from previous eras, even though the relevance of the view may have limited support or rationality in the present day. An example is the classic Great Man perspective that many students either implicitly or explicitly endorse. The opportunity to conclude that such an idea is irrational in contemporary times helps to prepare students to explore new ideas. Another way to encourage students to examine previous notions is through experiential activity. Taking course members through an outdoor challenge or ropes course may open up issues that would otherwise only be intellectualized in reading and discussion. For example, what happens when the facilitator suddenly silences a person who has been the key communicator or problem solver in an outdoor challenge experience? Typically, others begin to take more responsibility for the functions this person performed or the one silenced begins to explore other forms of less direct and obvious communication. This kind of experience may teach both more quickly and deeply.

Travel can have a profound impact in helping students explore previous notions of leadership and assumptions about the world around them. Travel could be to a community near the campus, in the region, across state lines, or international. The greater the difference in culture that students encounter, the greater difference the experience is likely to make in challenging students' previous ideas. Travel abroad can be particularly meaningful as a way to reduce the ongoing clutter of life and thereby expose students to experiences they would never have had otherwise. Sharon Parks (2000) indicates that "international travel can evoke deepened recognition of connection and interdependence" by "awakening curiosity, evoking awe, deepening compassion, informing the mind, and opening possibilities" (p. 185). This description conveys what happens when students shift from previous perspectives that may have allowed them to maintain comfortable isolation from the broader world around them. International or other travel that takes students out of familiar places forces them to question ideas of self-sufficiency. In order to succeed in new and foreign environments, students have to learn to be comfortable with and to accept help from others. For students who believe that leading is about strong, forceful experts who make things happen on their own, a brief interaction with a helpful stranger may trigger adopting a completely new perspective.

Seeing

Once downloading has taken place, we begin to get outside our own perspective, allowing us to see more accurately. Seeing more accurately includes both broadening our view and seeing the reality in greater detail. Assessment of students' talents, interests, and goals is one of the most useful ways to stimulate the process of seeing the world in a different way. From the resulting increase in self-awareness, students can see a clearer and more detailed picture of leadership and its dynamics.

Assessments related to different theoretical models are regularly integrated into conference presentations and classes. Recommendations on which ones to use vary and are usually based on whether or not the particular theory complements one's preferred approach to leadership. The Student Leadership Practices Inventory-self (Kouzes & Posner, 2005) has been validated in a special version for college students. The Myers Briggs Type Indicator (Myers & Briggs Foundation, 2006) is frequently used to increase the understanding of different personality types. The DiSC (Inscape Publishing, 2001) is used to explore characteristics of dominance, influence, steadiness, and conscientiousness related to leadership. The StrengthsQuest model (Gallup Organization, 2005) encourages reliance on enhancing strengths as a strategy for personal and leadership success. In addition to using assessment in specific contexts, creating a Leadership Assessment Center may help meet the broader needs for leadership assessment in all areas of educational practice. This could be done as a stand-alone service or it could be created in a cooperative venture with a campus counseling and testing center. Having leadership assessment available as an on-call service provides the opportunity for individuals or groups, outside of formal coursework or conferences, to benefit from ongoing assessment. An example of when this might be helpful includes when a faculty or staff member refers a student who by virtue of strong personality attributes may be struggling to sustain relationships. Or situations of conflict between students who are working on a joint project may warrant referral of the group by their adviser. Another example is in living groups in residence halls or fraternal organizations. If such groups wish to become better acquainted and authentic in their relationships, members might take independent assessments and then compare their results in a group interpretation. Assessment is a way of holding up the mirror for students so that they can see themselves more as others see them. Seeing others' perspectives and beginning to realize the different talents and gifts that everyone brings to leadership can be a powerful means of promoting leadership development. Instruments designed to assist students with career decision making may have broader applicability to other interests as well. As students seek to see the possibilities for leadership, having the opportunity to assess their degree of interest in certain fields in comparison to others may be instructive.

Another powerful way for students to begin to see the world more clearly and accurately is through community service or service-learning. Student participation in charity, philanthropy, and community service have been a part of the college environment for many decades. These forms of service have been couched in terms of social obligation, a way to give back to one's community. Charity, philanthropy, and service are often conceived as a responsibility of those who are privileged—to whom much is given, much is required. Although these ideas and origins of service have merit, service-learning assumes that students are more deeply engaged in the service and that their views of the world change as a result of the experience (Schroeder, Penner, Dovidio, & Piliavin, 1995).

Service-learning is a method to encourage students to look more carefully at the world around them, helping them to see it in greater detail and without preconceived notions. Some service-learning takes place in academic courses or as a complement to them. Regardless of whether credit is offered or not, an important distinction of service-learning compared to other forms of service is that learning from the experience is more intentional. For example, the church group that my youngest daughter attended while she was in high school took an alternative spring break trip to New York City. The trip was filled with a variety of experiences, one of which was the Midnight Run, an organization that sends vans throughout the city at midnight to deliver clothing, food, and other personal items to the homeless. Those participating in the service were involved in preparing for the run and interacted with those who were served through it. This particular experience deepened when Darbi began a conversation with one of the men she encountered during the night. She found that this man was college educated, intelligent, resourceful, full of hope, and eager for the next and more hopeful step in his life. This insight, contrasted with her previous notions, allowed her to see homelessness in a totally different way—as something that can happen to anyone and that can be solved through the provision of resources and opportunity. The experience of working with the Midnight Run was complemented by discussions among the adult counselors and the students, which allowed them to reflect on what they experienced so that they could download their previous ideas and begin to see the world in a different light. The critical points to reinforce as students embark in service-learning are that they must do so with deep respect for those being served, and that they should assume that both those being served and those who are serving are mutually engaged with each other. These conditions set the stage for students to interact meaningfully with diverse people and subsequently see the world in a different way.

Travel can also be utilized to stimulate students' clarity of vision, much like the alternative spring break mentioned above. Ecological trips may involve cleaning up degraded environmental areas. Service trips may include students from many campuses joining together in power-building periods for Habitat for Humanity. These experiences involve students in ways that allow them to see their world in more complex ways and teach them that there are other young people throughout the world devoted to helping address societal problems.

Orientation for new students in residence hall environments can help students see new and attractive opportunities as they begin collegiate life. Orientation can be conceived in ways that reinforce the importance of students seeing themselves as responsible for their own learning, as critically engaged in campus affairs, and as capable of leadership. Messages of this type are essential to students' seeing themselves as capable of constructing their own experience and taking charge of their own learning; such messages have a profound impact on student motivation. In many collegiate settings, certain students come to campus having had more privileges in leadership in high school and therefore expecting to have the same opportunity in college. These students can be encouraged to consider the possibility that when talent and interest are high, leadership is not about competition but is about joining together with others who have shared interests, all working to discover the leadership potential within themselves. Residence hall staff are some of the strongest influences in establishing the context for leadership learning. These staff should be encouraged to see themselves as part of the leadership learning staff of the campus. By doing so, residence hall staff can establish expectations of high involvement and shared leadership through the way they approach issues of residence hall environment, governance, and responsibility for behavior.

Independent research is another way to immerse students in seeing their world more accurately. Because of the individualized nature of these opportunities, students are able to identify areas of interest that they wish to explore and the methods of discovery that they prefer. When students have significant responsibility for their learning and when they engage with curiosity and openness, the potential depth of learning is enhanced considerably. A number of leadership programs involve peers in the analyses and design of programs. This kind of involvement not only allows students to provide new or enriched opportunities for their peers but also to see themselves as competent and capable, a mind-set that enhances their own learning.

The Duke University Hart Leadership Program is a particularly good example of the power of deep engagement that stimulates a shift in the way students see the world. The Hart Leadership Program curriculum embraces three commitments: immersion, critical reflection, and "going public." Immersion involves students in directly engaging a real problem at the university or in the surrounding community. Critical reflection involves the dimensions of personal (fostering personal growth and awareness), interpersonal (including mentor relationships), and academic (increasing knowledge of systems, patterns, and operating concepts) learning. Such engagement captivates students and stimulates their critical thinking. Once they begin to see the world in greater depth and detail, they share their new realizations with others by "going

public" in open forum presentations. The magic of going public
is that, as they are challenged through dialogue with peers and
others, they examine even more deeply the questions they had
and the initial conclusions they have drawn. This kind of experience helps them see the potential to contribute to a greater common good, which is analogous to "sensing" the possibilities of real
change that I describe next.

Sensing

Sensing is an evolutionary process, and responding to it functions
much like a magnet, drawing out our commitment and talent. Conclusions about what is to be done are very tentative at this point
because we are just beginning to see new possibilities for actions
we might take. It is important that this process of discovery about
the world and our role in improving it be approached with patience
and wonder, rather than urgency and insistence. The examples that
follow have the potential to open students to new possibilities for
a deeper kind of leadership. Student response at this level is likely
to vary; some will welcome the chance to broaden their worldview,
and others will be uncomfortable with the perceived pressure of
finding their place in the world.

One powerful opportunity for sensing is the LeaderShape Institute. Beginning in 1986 as a program targeting fraternity men,
LeaderShape has evolved into a program for students from a variety of backgrounds and experiences and is available at national
and campus-based sites throughout the country. The Leader-
Shape Institute is a six-day intensive leadership learning experience that takes place with a small group of a maximum of sixty
participants in an immersion retreat. Trained individuals known
as Lead Facilitators guide the Institute and work with a group
of Cluster Facilitators who in turn work intensely with students
throughout the six-day period. The curriculum at all LeaderShape
Institutes is the same and is revised based on rigorous evaluation
each year. One of the primary outcomes of the Institute is that

students formulate a vision of a cause or project they care about and will commit to pursue as part of their immediate collegiate and eventual life experiences. This vision is, in essence, the result of participants coming to sense the possibilities for their contribution to the world. There are numerous examples of LeaderShape participants who have continued to pursue their visions while modifying and shaping their approach as their life experiences unfold. The Institute's commitment is to start a lifelong process that shapes young adults' lives around commitments to transformative vision and integrity in their actions.

One of the challenges that some colleges face is helping students break out of the environmental cocoon that becomes so familiar and comfortable for them. Even on campuses in thriving and diverse urban communities, the tendency to seek comfortable spaces may keep students from experiencing environments that challenge them to see their role in the world differently. Conferences that are away from campus and take students into environments that are foreign to them can begin a process of stimulating students to consider, or sense, other possibilities. One particular conference, the National Black Student Leadership Conference, is offered annually in Virginia. This professional-oriented conference draws a large audience of students and advisers from throughout the nation, and it provides a setting that is unusual in most students' lives. Students come expecting to be challenged through the opportunity to see and meet educators, politicians, artists, and activists who are changing the world through their actions. The messages that students cannot help but derive from this experience are about potential, critical mass, and stewardship of one's own and others' futures. This experience stimulates the consideration of what contribution each and every one of the participants can make to the betterment of those who have suffered discrimination. Another example of this kind of opportunity was the Inter-Faith Dialogue retreat at Princeton University in the spring of 2005. This conference, offered to diverse teams of students who were committed to fostering interfaith dialogue on their campuses, provided a dramatic picture of what campuses could be like if they really were able to achieve respect among students from different religious backgrounds.

In a classroom setting, advanced leadership courses can stimulate the process of sensing possibilities for change through leadership. Especially when these courses involve group projects focused on change, community-based research, or other team activities, these courses help students realize the influence they have in shaping a world that is more fair, equitable, and caring. Returning to the example of Duke's Hart Leadership Program, the Enterprising Leadership Incubator stems from the introductory course during which students identified promising ideas that could be addressed in the future. The Enterprising Leadership Incubator pushes the initial ideas deeper by encouraging students to think big as they attempt to effect change in organizations and community action. When resources inhibit the change initiatives and learning that comes from it, seed money can be made available to assist students with their initiatives.

Sensing new possibilities for oneself can also be bound to one of the dilemmas of both new and mature programs: how to maintain and renew momentum in campus programs. As new research and models unfold, we become aware of innovative processes that can foster leadership. In order to stay aware of these developments and nurture the potential among a critical mass of leadership colleagues, it is important to offer a mechanism to draw those who have the ability to advance leadership learning into an ongoing conversation. One of the ways this could be done is through establishing a group dedicated to mutual learning that pushes the boundaries of leadership learning through shared responsibility for the process. The Learning Partnerships Model (Baxter Magolda, 2004) is a useful way of conceptualizing such a group. This model advocates that all those involved be seen as both learners and teachers, that knowledge is situated in their experiences, and that learning is the mutual construction of meaning. The mutual construction of meaning is particularly powerful because it recognizes that as students, faculty, and staff, we all help create meaning informed by our diverse experiential, cultural, and environmental backgrounds. With these assumptions, new and experienced staff, graduate students, and undergraduate peer leaders could work together to make sure that innovative ideas are regularly infused through the leadership learning opportunities on the campus. A leadership learning community could be a way to sense different possibilities in the design of leadership programs while demonstrating that processes are available that allow us to see and sense potential opportunities that we might otherwise never consider.

Presencing

The phase from which this model draws its name, presencing, reflects a moment, a period of time, or progressive experiences when we begin to understand that we really have found worthy work to which we are willing to dedicate ourselves. Finding this real purpose is likely to begin with tentative and even timid pronouncement of what matters to us. As we become more comfortable with our convictions, we become more authentic in the declaration of our beliefs. The process of discovering deeper purpose could be likened to walking a tightrope—a process full of breathless and uncertain moments at first. In the company of others who support us in these moments, we find our balance and thus grow more confident and effective in expressing our own beliefs.

Having a mentor to accompany students on the journey of presence is particularly important during this phase of the model. Ideally, a mentor would be available throughout the young adulthood period. However, when students begin to sense the possibilities for their own lives, reach out to role models, and start to proclaim their convictions, they require a mentor. The concept of mentor-protégé relationships has been popularized in many leadership and other types of programs. Some of these programs represent no more than acquaintanceship or coaching. To have a real mentor-protégé relationship is very powerful. I encourage you to reserve the use of these words for these important times.

Sharon Parks's *Big Questions, Worthy Dreams* (2000) addresses how young adults come to understand themselves and develop a sense of faith. It relies heavily on notions of developing relationships with mentors who are good company on the road of discovery. Parks proposed that developing faith is closely aligned with the process that William Perry (1998) described in his groundbreaking book, *Forms of Ethical and Intellectual Development in the College Years: A Scheme*. In her adaptation, Parks explains that young adults pass through the following stages on the journey toward purpose:

1. Authority-bound, dualistic

2. Unqualified relativism

3. Probing commitment

4. Tested commitment

5. Convictional commitment

I previously proposed in Chapter Five that there is a similarity between the Presence model and Perry's progressive phases of intellectual and ethical development. With Parks's language and focus on conviction, it is even easier to see the relationship to the unfolding experience of discovering conviction.

Parks indicates that young adults who are either authority-bound and dualistic or view the world through the lens of unqualified relativism are really not developmentally ready to address questions of conviction. Having an authority-bound perspective is a natural part of development and reflects the experiences of earlier childhood, where the security of knowing and the predictability of authority are so important. Likewise, unqualified relativism reflects a natural opening from a world previously viewed through dualistic frames. Young adults who see the world with unqualified relativism do not see the need or relevance of conviction in their own lives.

It is probing conviction that begins to provide real opportunities to engage with mentors.

If we are lucky, protégés will seek us out as they begin to look for deeper purposes for their lives. There is frequently an acquaintanceship that precedes this deeper phase that has allowed the protégé to see the potential for a more substantial relationship with the mentor. As I have experienced the beginnings of probing conviction with students, it has frequently come at moments of confusion, frustration, or disillusionment. A former student whom I advised and with whom I stayed in contact when she went to law school worked very hard, graduated at the top of her class, and joined a corporate law firm in a major city. At first she was exhilarated by the work, the people, and the challenge. Eventually, she began to see political dynamics, sexism, and lifestyle implications that made her increasingly uncomfortable. But she struggled to comprehend how she could possibly give up a lifetime dream, ignore all that work, and deal with the debt she had acquired while moving toward a newly discovered dream. I had numerous other opportunities to advise and encourage this talented young woman, but the moment of truth—the time of the deepest search for conviction in her life to this point—was when she stood at the threshold of these questions. At this moment we deepened our previous relationship and moved into the mutual and searching world of a mentor-protégé relationship.

Probing conviction, or the initial experience with presence, is likely to be characterized by a tentative expression of purpose. This delicate moment is the ideal time for mentors to help young adults anchor the vision they have of themselves or, in Parks's language, to "beckon the self into being" (2000, p. 81). The initial exploration of deeper commitments is a threshold experience that allows young adults to explore their imagination for how the world could be and then begin living into that possibility.

During periods of deep discovery, some young adults become discouraged because of denigration they experience at the hands of those who dismiss the possibilities of transformative change. Finding mentor relationships or being involved in a community that serves a mentor function for its members is critical if the flame is to be kept alive at these times. Whether it is an individual or community attribute, to be mentored is to have one's big questions and aspirations welcomed. Three practices could be cultivated in order to welcome these big questions (Parks, 2000, pp. 154–156):

> Practice of the Hearth: Hearth places are where we are warmed in both body and soul, are made comfortable, and tend to linger.
>
> Practice of the Table: The table is where we learn to share, to wait, to accommodate, to be grateful.
>
> Practice of the Commons: The commons helps us to stand with each other through interrelatedness and belonging, even when we may come from very different places.

It seems that these practices could be useful for those who want to make it clear that they are open to protégés. Creating hearth could be accomplished by being less hurried and by becoming more peaceful in our interactions. Creating table would result from curiosity about students, their lives, and what they seek to accomplish. Creating commons as a mentor would mean supporting students when they stand up for an ideal, even though it may contradict our own views or those of the institution that employs us. Hearth, table, and commons can be interpreted in so many different ways when we look at our individual behaviors. The three practices could also be applied to living groups, to organizations, and to joint initiatives in which students are involved. Attention to hearth in a living group would mean ensuring that there is a quiet communal place where students can comfortably be with each other in reflection. Attention to table in a student organization might be as simple as encouraging respectful meeting processes that demonstrate a willingness to accommodate one another's ideas. Attention to commons in student initiatives would mean connecting students who have conflicting, related, or cooperative interests. All of these are relevant and should be taken seriously in order for students to find individual mentors and communities to support them when they are exploring probing conviction questions.

The most important point I hope to make is that if presence and an authentic conviction around which to form our lives is to be nurtured and sustained, the initial and tentative expression of it must be welcomed either individually by a mentor or by a community that can offer a similar function. Being intentional and concentrating in deeper ways could result in amazing revelations for our students that spur them to greater accomplishments than they or we could ever imagine. Indeed, this kind of potential was captured by Donald Cutler (personal communication, December 7, 1991), the minister who delivered the eulogy for Esther Lloyd-Jones, when he stated, "Through her accomplishments one sees what a frequent mentor she was, and she bore the stuff of all great mentors, that they are not competitive but rather luxuriate in the accomplishments of their protégés." This statement is so much a part of the mentor-protégé dynamic. The mentor knows the potential in the protégé, so much so that she not only accepts but also hopes that the protégé will eclipse the mentor's own accomplishments. This is good company for the road toward conviction in one's life.

Civic engagement opportunities could provide other interesting, and perhaps related, opportunities to enhance the discernment of presence in leadership learning. Many authors and speakers have raised concern in recent literature about young adults' commitment to civic affairs (Ehrlich, 1999; Putman, 2000). Civic matters require resolution through community. As a way of thinking about these community concerns, one might adopt the idea of civitas captured in the practice of the table, a place that requires sharing, waiting, accommodation, and gratefulness (Parks, 2000). Through a campus leadership learning initiative focusing on civic engagement and relying on these principles, processes like monetary and physical space allocation would emphasize sharing and accommodation for the greater good rather than competition and winner-take-all. Celebrations and acknowledgment of students who have made important leadership contributions to the campus might also look different, both in terms of who is recognized and how the tributes are offered and accepted.

The idea of presence epitomizes the first half of the definition that I previously proposed as a foundation for deeper leadership: conviction in action. The declaration of purpose is likely to be tentative at first, but as confidence is gained, these provisional convictions turn into deeper and longer-term commitments and eventually a willingness to act. It is the willingness to act that draws us into the next phase: envisioning.

Envisioning

Envisioning involves beginning the process of pulling ideas, resources, and people together to achieve the intended outcome: the vision. Being deeply centered and present in leadership makes envisioning both easy and difficult. On one hand, leadership informed by deep conviction is easy because it feels natural, is highly motivating, and is ultimately the work we cannot help but do. On the other hand, deeper leadership is difficult because it can easily be misunderstood as too grandiose or too much of an imposition on others. This tension between the proclamation of what matters and helping students understand the critical importance of listening to and incorporating the responses of others is likely to require special attention.

The LeaderShape Institute, mentioned previously as a possible initiative to help students sense their greater potential, actually has its greatest impact after the six-day program has concluded. The curriculum includes a focus on day seven and beyond as a way of encouraging participants to remember the importance of what they have learned and putting the lessons into action. One of the first implications of envisioning for LeaderShape participants is that, once they have identified something to which they will dedicate themselves, they begin to realize that few goals truly worth accomplishing can be tackled alone. The envisioning phase is where leadership really begins to happen. Students' perception of what it takes to be successful in pursuing their dreams can either serve as an attractor for others or push them away. Envisioning will attract others when students invite input, listen carefully, and incorporate both ideas and additional mutually beneficial aspirations into a plan. However, if students insist on the rightness of their views and if they force prescriptive ideas and strategies on others, they undermine the collective process that allows others to envision with them. Understanding this dynamic is difficult for some students, especially if their personalities are strong and they are used to having leadership privilege from previous experiences. Many students who have had positional roles, such as president or chairperson, assume that the authority they held and the way they used it to influence others resulted in their success. But the systemic and lasting changes these same students now seek cannot be achieved through the same processes they used before. They have to explore other models in order to become effective. One of the models I frequently use to help students understand this dynamic is Ronald Heifetz's adaptive leadership (1994). As I explained in Chapter Four, adaptive leadership is most appropriate when the solution to a question or problem is unclear or unknown. This is likely to be the state of affairs for many of the big questions students wish to address once they have explored the presence phase. Leadership in this circumstance is a matter of holding the question up to others and engaging with them as the group collectively explores the tensions surrounding the question. Leaders do not have to have all the answers; rather, they must engage others in the work of discerning possible strategies and methods that have the potential to be effective. Understanding and learning to lead in this way may be difficult for students who have just discovered something about which they care a great deal; support groups, consultations, and resource centers could prove helpful to students during this phase. Fortunately, students at this point have such deep convictions in their purpose that there are seldom problems with motivation. Students who have been awakened will do practically anything in their power to progress when they care enough about the goal.

Small group initiatives or seminars can be very beneficial to students during the envisioning phase because they allow for an intimacy unlikely in other formats. Two kinds of groups in which I have worked over the years have titles that convey their purpose: Inspired Annoyance and Kindred Spirits. In the Inspired Annoyance noncredit seminar that I have periodically conducted, the purpose is to find students who have a depth of conviction about something but have no support group to use as a sounding board in pursuing it. The analogy of oysters creating pearls served as the basis for this seminar group. By reflecting on the analogy, students gain greater acceptance of the discomforts of big questions (the grain of sand that enters an oyster), learn to respond affirmatively to the annoyance (the outside coating of the grain), and thus create outcomes of great value (the pearl). A particularly useful text for the Inspired Annoyance seminar is Parker Palmer's *The Active Life* (1990). I have typically used each of the successive chapters of Palmer's book as a way of proposing the importance of balancing contemplative and active practice in leadership. The Kindred Spirits retreat was sponsored jointly with the Campus Ministry Center for several years. Its purpose was similar to that of Inspired Annoyance in that it was targeted for students who had made initial commitments to deep leadership work but who could benefit from having kindred to share their journey. Kindred Spirits was a weekend reflective retreat, but sometimes involved both preparatory and follow-up sessions.

Helping students envision action based on their conviction can also be advanced in students' experience through the community-based research method (Stoecker, 2004), in which faculty or staff guide students in completing academic projects in teams. The Hart Program's Enterprising Leadership Incubator is a good example of this. Through community-based research, course instructors and students identify community concerns and then students participate in research that deepens their understanding of the problem. Eventually, students collaborate with community members to formulate plans for and take action toward addressing the problem. This is truly envisioning in its fullest sense—engaging a question that has no clear answer with research and analyses that draws multiple stakeholders together in its resolution.

Residential groups that have self-governance as a significant part of their purpose are also ideal environments through which to explore the dynamics of envisioning. Many college students today have never really participated in a community that lives by democratic practices and that takes responsibility for the quality of life in the community. Fraternal organizations have this as part of their historic tradition, but most have lost sight of this notion in their contemporary form. Residence halls were at least partially created to provide students with the opportunity to take responsibility for their own affairs as a way of teaching democratic living. Unfortunately, concerns over liability and attention to consumer service have undermined the self-governance goal. In both fraternal organizations and living groups, a commitment to envisioning and then living as a real democratic community could be revived as very helpful leadership learning opportunities. Such opportunities would help students acquire both leadership capacity as well as an understanding of what healthy and engaged communities entail.

Carnegie Mellon University offers an ongoing annual event called the Syzygy Conference. The word syzygy is like synergy, but stronger. Syzygy reflects a yoking together of those with common ideas. The Syzygy Conference draws students together around common commitments to personal values, visioning, collaboration, and networking. The theme for Syzygy 2006, "Align for Action," encouraged sharing ideas and collaborating to create positive change. A conference conceived in this spirit could not help but aid students as they envision how to put their convictions into action.

Enacting

Enacting takes what we envision, breaks it down into initial steps, and includes acting in the instant to test the effectiveness of our strategies. These initial steps become prototypes for subsequent and more substantial action directed toward fulfilling the vision. Leadership learning that provides opportunities for students to enact their commitments results in greater institutional capacity that addresses questions and concerns important to the community while at the same time enhancing learning itself. As students begin to act, they become a volunteer force for the campus and community, addressing needs and drawing other students into greater participation. Almost all broad campus models that support leadership learning have some limitation in resources. By involving peers, the available human resources expand to respond to the emerging needs.

Students who will benefit most at the enacting level are those who are on a journey, or have shifted, to a new level in their leadership identity. As previously described in Chapter Four, Komives and her colleagues (2005) discovered that students eventually move to a "leadership differentiated" phase that enables them to embrace others, involve them, share with them, and value the contributions of all those who are dedicated to advancing a common vision for change. Students who have these beliefs are infectious in their advocacy for others to engage in leadership. In fact, one of the primary leadership objectives for these students is to make more students aware of the pleasure and fulfillment that is possible by learning about and participating in leadership learning.

For students who have ideas that they wish to pursue, three resources that are likely to be most important are training and information resources, monetary resources, and a place to pursue the work with others. Students who have discovered the power of conviction in their own lives will many times find their own paths to these resources, but it is essential to ensure that training, financial assistance, and physical space are available and that students of all backgrounds, experiences, and perspectives know of their availability.

Regarding training needs, students may or may not have had experiences through which they learned basic skills such as organizing and facilitating meetings, budgetary processes, event-planning strategies, and campus administrative and bureaucratic structures. Although this kind of training may routinely be available through conferences, brochures, and handouts, there may also be a need to provide a responsive leadership training initiative that encourages students to assess their needs and request assistance on topics of interest at suitable times and places. With the technology available on most campuses, such a responsive system could be placed online with staff or paraprofessionals working with organizations to fulfill their requests. The greatest advantage of such a system is that students will have intrinsic motivation to learn what they need to learn, a condition that is likely to significantly enhance comprehension and retention.

Regarding monetary resources, most campuses have student government funding allocations that can be tapped. However, the broad and innovative nature of the initiatives that some students wish to pursue, especially if they are stimulated by the deeper leadership journey I advocate here, may require access to other sources. An incubator approach that supports innovation and change could be taken with this kind of funding. This would be most effective when there are no existing structures and processes to support their initiatives. Once students have completed a plan, they could come to a student or faculty-student committee to request support for their work. In my travels I have found that this model is already in places as far-flung as the United States, Canada, and France. The interesting thing is that the process is sometimes not recognized as a primary means of stimulating leadership capacity. It would be so easy in the cases where the funding mechanism already exists to add the twist, "And what did you learn about leadership as a result of your experience?"

Relating to and complementing the provision of monetary resources, it is important to provide physical space, or a crossroads, for students who seek to make a difference and are striving to test their ideas as they enact them through leadership. There may be a particular need to focus on students who have social activism goals when it comes to this space. Groups that advocate social change are sometimes found only at the fringes of the campus. In these cases, it is important, and relatively easy, to provide a meeting, gathering, and basic office space that allows them the same privilege of resources that more conventional groups receive (Meyers, 2006). The location of a social activism center is a delicate issue and needs careful consideration. On one hand, these groups may prefer to have private space separate from other groups. On the other hand, to place them somewhere else may inadvertently send a marginalizing message.

When considering the idea of providing a gathering place for social activism groups, one way of stirring up the context for leadership learning would be to find a location that provides a designated space or office for collaborative leadership. The common space between social activism and other student clubs and organizations could help students discover that they actually have more in common than they thought and that the leadership learning each is pursuing is mutually informing and reinforcing.

When thinking about students who are eager to enact their commitments, some interesting surprises can occur. I had a particularly wonderful encounter with a first-year student who was entertaining the prospect of leaving the university. He expressed his intent to a friend who suggested that he might want to speak with me before he left. The student made an appointment, showed up in my office, and proceeded to express a litany of dissatisfactions with fellow students and the lack of active learning on the campus. I spoke with the student only a couple of times at first, but I encouraged him to enact his own commitments by listening carefully to others, getting involved in some initial leadership programs, and checking back with me. The result was that he learned more about himself, became more effective, and realized that there were plenty of opportunities for active learning. Most important, he discovered that students were the most appropriate source for much of this learning. He became an advocate for others to be involved and proceeded to build new strategies and methods that invited students to explore their own convictions in leadership and put them into action. This student single-handedly became one of the most effective leadership program "staff" that we ever had. He not only stayed at the university but also became involved in ways that transformed his experience and that of others.

Enacting involves taking one's awareness of a need, one that is informed by critical experiences and analysis, sharing it with others in ways that invite them to shape it for their own purposes, and beginning the initial steps to bring about change. This progression leads eventually to embodying the change that we seek to create.

Embodying

The final phase of the Presence model is the result of all the deeper leadership work that faculty, staff, students, and community members alike pursue. Embodying our dreams, whoever and wherever we are, is important because there are those who have not done the inner and deep work of leadership who sometimes pose as if they have. I do not mean this judgmentally or critically. Where we are is where we are, and I have no doubt that there are many individuals who believe they have pursued the inner work. The unfortunate part of that is that their behavior shows otherwise. Arrogance, imposition of will, demeaning others, dishonesty, and other attributes are all clues that the deeper learning of leadership has not yet been part of their experience. Trusting our own intuition about this is important. Our intuition about others' depth of commitment should always be explored while maintaining a generous and nonjudgmental stance. The important part is that we also need opportunities in leadership learning that help more of us embody deeper leadership, and we need ways to celebrate it in each other.

One of the most available and probably underutilized sources of embodied leadership are faculty advisers to student clubs, organizations, and honoraries. Most campuses require that student organizations have faculty or staff advisers, but many also allow the signature on the form to be the end of the involvement. Giving advisers mental models on how to enhance students' learning about leadership could pay off in so many different ways. The Learning Partnerships Model (Baxter Magolda, 2004) is one useful framework for fostering professional development among faculty and staff advisers. It is relatively easy to reach an agreement that student learning could be enhanced—and our pleasure in working with them increased—if students had internal belief systems, an established internal identity, and a conviction that learning takes place through mutual relationships. However, this is not the way most of our students come to us; Baxter Magolda found that, indeed, this view of learning is frequently not achieved until some time after the collegiate experience. Baxter Magolda and her coauthors do outline ways of moving toward this ideal. For example, the programs that implement the Learning Partnerships model have been influential in supporting students in the movement toward more complex and responsible constructions of their learning. Contrasted with workshops on legal responsibilities and policy briefings, this kind of approach in adviser development would help faculty and staff understand the power of cocurricular involvement and the importance of encouraging students along their journey toward deeper leadership potential.

Recognition of students, faculty, staff, and alumni who make unusual and transformative contributions to the campus and community is another important dimension to embodying deeper leadership. Recognition can sometimes deteriorate into popularity votes that only reward visibility. By contrast, recognition of leadership contributions should be as authentic and deeply felt as possible. Some campuses offer a series of meetings where, in addition to recognition, faculty, staff, and students reflect on their educational journey. Such a series would help to focus on the journey of those who embody deeper leadership rather than focusing primarily on their achievements.

Another mostly unrecognized opportunity to facilitate embodied leadership is to help students achieve their dreams by applying to graduate or professional school and especially through applications for fellowships and awards that honor their work. The shock on students' faces when they are encouraged to apply for a Truman Scholarship, a Marshall, a Rhodes, or others is priceless. The delight and humility that simultaneously appear on their faces is sure proof that they are deserving of this kind of recognition. The process, and the occasions when students achieve these awards, are profoundly fulfilling when those receiving the awards have walked the path of deeper leadership.

Finally, selecting speakers who exemplify deeper leadership provides a powerful way for institutions to embody desired leadership qualities. When institutions carefully select campus speakers for their character and their service, they symbolically convey what they value in leadership learning.

These examples demonstrate different ways in which educators can use the unfolding phases of the Presence model as a purposeful framework for comprehensive leadership learning. There could be many more examples, depending on the culture, resources, and desires of any given campus. The most important commitment of these programs and initiatives is that they provide opportunities for students to explore the personal journey toward deeper leadership. When looking at presence as a programmatic framework, there is one other phase that might be important.

Renewing

Perhaps there should be one more "ing" to round out the Presence model. This term was already implied in the conversation between Ken Wilber and Otto Scharmer (2003). It is "renewing." Learning and adopting the stages of presence in our lives create a way of renewing us throughout life's experience. As we explore ever deeper awareness of the role we are called to play, and as we revisit the cycle of presence, we are renewed and reborn in our potential. This also takes place at the organizational and programmatic level through assessment and intentional efforts for continuous improvement. We now turn to flow and oscillation, the other dimensions of the deeper leadership model.

Flow

I have proposed that deeper leadership has to begin with students— with their concerns, their interests, and their convictions. Once students know what they want and they understand the framework for progressing toward their visions, they will be more open to learning and willing to acquire the tools that will allow them to be effective. These are the very same conditions that make flow possible.

As noted in Chapter Five, flow is a condition where individuals and groups are able to achieve goals far beyond their typical and expected performance levels. Flow involves a level of attention and focus that provides the conditions necessary to achieve peak performance, not as a matter of competition with someone else but simply for the joy of doing one's best in the company of other great performers.

To demonstrate the principles of flow, I deliberately chose one of the most complex organizations present on most college campuses: the student government. The organizational structure may vary from campus to campus, but almost all colleges have a student government. This is the organization most often profiled or criticized in the student or local newspaper, and therefore is likely to be the organization that most visibly reinforces or contradicts the purposes of leadership learning.

Presence, flow, and oscillation start with the identification of work worth doing. Therein lies the problem. Student government on most college campuses is an ongoing organization assumed to exist from year to year. The organization does not have to renew itself, other than by electing new representatives, and unless something happens to stir student advocacy or activism, it usually remains an inert entity. Sometimes an incident occurs on campus. Fees are raised or a favorite professor is denied tenure. These can be enough to spark intense interest among student government leadership, but only for the short term. If student government is to have the opportunity to strive for real accomplishment, it needs to have a view of itself for the long term. One possibility for establishing student government that is consistently productive, contributes much to the campus, and is sustainable involves encouraging the positional student leaders to adopt the ultimate purpose of demonstrating how democracy can work and how it serves its citizen constituents. This is a broad goal and one not easy to achieve. In fact, with the scrutiny of student media and the inevitable conflicts of interest that arise, student government is probably one of the most challenging student leadership roles available on the campus, clearly qualifying for the conditions identified in Csikszentmihaly's research (1993)—highly challenging goals that are just a little beyond our capability and hard, but not impossible, to reach.

If a campus student government could begin to understand itself as the teaching laboratory for democracy, conditions could begin to improve. Then the other five variables of the flow model could be used to guide the organization and its members.

Concentration

The collegiate years are full of excitement, adjustments, and discovery. Especially because these disorienting qualities are part of all students' experiences, it is important to encourage student government to concentrate on focused and accomplishable goals that captivate them. This is an organizational role-modeling opportunity, demonstrating to other organizations and to students at large that to be effective, any individual or entity has to set priorities and stick with them. Students need to be able to concentrate their attention and to feel that they are competent and can excel when they do.

Absorption

There are few things that absorb us more than the ideas or objects we create. One of the great advantages of student government is that it is free to establish new and different priorities every year. It also has the opportunity to establish new committees, task forces, and clubs, or organizations. These are all potential opportunities to involve the immediate officers and members of student government as well as the many other students who will then have the chance to participate. Students can also experience absorption when a great challenge is placed before them. Giving students real responsibility to help draft responses to campus problems can provide absorption opportunities, and also just may unearth a solution that faculty or staff would not have considered.

Deep Involvement

Cooperative or collaborative experiences frequently require deeper involvement than we anticipate, but they also provide the potential for deeper fulfillment as goals are reached through enhancing relationships and organization connections. Student government can be the broker for important campuswide or interorganizational efforts. As these efforts take hold, those involved deepen their investment and involvement as well as discover the excitement of really making tangible progress toward a goal.

Joy

Student government leaders frequently need a lot of help when it comes to preserving the joy and humor in their work. Opportunities to get together socially, to have surprise acknowledgments, and to receive appreciative notes from faculty and administration can all contribute to a deeper sense of joy through their leadership.

Sense of Accomplishment

Attempting to achieve feats that appear impossible is practically the definition of student government. There are many challenges and opportunities, and one of the key responsibilities of the adviser is to help the participants remember what they are accomplishing and to remind them of the long and arduous work contributed by students who came before them.

Helping student government to be more effective is a powerful means to demonstrate how well democracy and civic engagements can function. Instead of using the "in'trick'acies" of Roberts Rules of Order to win through tactics rather than reason, meetings could be redesigned to encourage those who have been marginalized or alienated to get involved. Student government is real because it addresses substantive issues on campus while at the same time demonstrating the efficacy of civic engagement. The advisory role in such a student government would then become one of fostering more authentic leadership, engaging students in the process of real governance, and challenging them to push themselves to the kind of learning that achieves the higher performance made possible by striving for flow.

On a more individual level, the flow conditions of concentration, absorption, deep involvement, joy, and accomplishment can be used to help students understand the dynamics of their academic and cocurricular work. These are conditions that students could create for themselves if they were aware of how powerful these flow conditions are in supporting peak performance. One student with whom I worked several years ago initially frustrated me because she was so selective in her involvements. I thought of her talent and how much she had to offer. Accordingly, she was consistently at the top of my list when I was asked by others on campus for student nominees to committees, task forces, and special projects. I came to realize later that she was not rejecting or avoiding involvement but was simply concentrating her immense talent and energy toward a purpose that had become her identity. She was absorbed in her aspirations and was highly successful in her final accomplishments. I suspect that if I were to talk to her today and share the concept of flow and the conditions of concentration, absorption, deep involvement, joy, and accomplishment, she would be able to tell me exactly how she shaped her intellectual and campus involvement so that she could be a peak performer in the areas she most prized. This template for high performance could become the grist for conversation between protégés and their mentors. It could also be used as a way to help students plan and pursue their curricular and cocurricular involvement while in college.

One of the most important ways flow experiences can be reinforced among students is by identifying someone or some group as the "go-to" person for those who have innovative and different ideas. Whether this is a formal role or is a dispersed commitment made among many faculty and staff makes little difference. The point is that students who discover conviction in their lives need a go-to person who can help them find ways to pursue their passions. Study abroad, cultural understanding, scientific discovery, social change, artistic expression, and many other endeavors are sometimes difficult to launch but, if supported, can turn into peak performance that is amazing.

Oscillation

Helping students achieve variability in their experiences would add significantly to their self-discovery process and would make greater creativity and innovation possible. I am not referring here to the typical rhythm of undergraduate life involving intense study and preparation punctuated with periods of social activity and then complete exhaustion. Oscillation is the movement back and forth between acting and reflecting as a discipline, allowing us interludes to create new and innovative ideas that we can then test in practice.

There are a variety of ways to infuse oscillation into students' lives. Examples include journaling, music, pleasure reading, writing, service, or exercise. Incorporating one or more of these disciplines can provide a renewing breath on a daily basis. In my own experience, I have committed to an exercise period of about an hour every day. When I am at home, I usually complete this on a stationary bicycle while reading. When I am away, I walk and either listen to music or simply let my mind wander to absorb the environment around me. In both of these cases, the renewing interlude is both physical and intellectual, energizing my day and stimulating creative exploration of possibilities I never considered.

There are a number of campuses that have created new kinds of reflective or spiritual spaces on their campuses. These are different from the chapels that have been on many campuses for a number of years; these are spaces for faith exploration, questioning, privacy, and renewal. Wellesley College in Massachusetts established an Office of Religious and Spiritual Life in 1993 and has become a model for private institutions in providing special opportunities for spiritual journey. Pennsylvania State University more recently established the Frank and Sylvia Pasquerilla Spiritual Center, the largest spiritual life center at any public university in the United States. Penn State's president, Dr. Graham Spanier, lauded the opening of the Center as a visual confirmation of Penn State's "tradition of supporting those students who are searching for an inner light" and who have "an increasing desire to find meaning and purpose" (Spanier, 2006). This statement affirms so clearly the importance of using spiritual, interfaith programs and facilities as necessary and purposeful oscillations in students' experiences.

Students can also benefit from oscillation over the course of months or the entire academic year. Retreats or service weekends can serve as renewing interludes. As I came to discover from observing students studying abroad, being in another country, away from familiar settings and supports, can be a wonderful stimulus to reconsider former ways of thinking. Independent research or a senior thesis may also provide oscillation back and forth between intense and purposeful work and periods of waiting for review and feedback. The oscillation of independent creative work and the guidance of a faculty sponsor can help a student gain new perspective and insight. Rather than seeing feedback as critique, might it be more productively viewed as the interlude that stimulates deeper thinking?

Such programs as the Inspired Annoyance seminar, which I mentioned earlier when discussing the envisioning phase of presencing, could also be very helpful to students as a part of their oscillation between activity and reflection. The cycle of the seminar, which included reading, discussion, and reflection on a weekly basis, allowed students to actively explore and personally contemplate the nagging questions we all have. This cycle took on an oscillation of its own as students began to realize the importance of the three elements of reading, discussion, and reflection.

Independent reading for credit or for personal enrichment can provide opportunities for individual students who seek or could be encouraged to look at oscillating experiences in their undergraduate lives. Over time, I have had the good fortune to work with numerous students who were interested in pursuing dialogue about purpose in their lives. I have welcomed the opportunity to work with these students in mutual reading programs. The format that I have generally followed is to dedicate ourselves to reading articles or a book together while maintaining discussions every other week or so. The preparation for the discussions and our meetings added intensity for both of us, and the interlude between the meetings provided opportunity to quietly reflect on what we were reading and learning. These experiences deepened our relationships while providing the opportunity to learn through oscillating acutely productive and reflective periods.

Another possibility for oscillation over a longer period of time is the compilation of a student portfolio, one of the primary methods I previously recommended as a powerful assessment strategy. Student involvement or leadership portfolios have been around for a long time, previously in hard copy and now more often in digital format. The purpose of portfolios is sometimes conveyed as a way to document involvement and leadership for prospective employers. However, the more influential and developmental implication is that creation and revision of student portfolios can serve as a way to stimulate oscillation back and forth between students' activities and their reflections on what they are learning. Especially when complemented with mentor-protégé pairings, a portfolio can become a road map for the student's college years, reflecting the depth of experience but accentuating the learning outcomes that are so very important. A portfolio could also include a personal leadership philosophy that students write and rewrite as their views change. Finally, a portfolio might be used to encourage students to identify experiences that will contribute to leadership learning, thus serving as a catalyst to be more purposeful. Once the experience takes place, students could be encouraged to analyze the degree to which the experience met their expectations and helped them learn what they wanted to learn.

Another experience related to leadership learning that may be best experienced as an oscillating theme throughout the undergraduate years is diversity education. Many campuses are finding that diversity education faces more and more resistance as a focused part of undergraduate education. Although the courses are useful, the students who usually take them need them the least. When campus events with a diversity theme are scheduled, the auditorium is predictably filled with the program's advocates. The sad reality is that diversity education has become routine, and students' responses are disappointing. Might diversity education be more attractive, and therefore more effective, if it is infused into events with other foci rather than targeted in special events and speakers? Cultural proficiency would then become an "oscillating" theme through a number of experiences, turning them into opportunities to foster a climate of cultural proficiency among all leadership program participants (Lindsay, Robins, & Terrel, 2003).

Creating a Campus Culture That Affirms Presence, Flow, and Oscillation

I have come to believe that the most influential leadership learning is the product of a campus culture that values and unabashedly lauds the importance of such learning and that communicates to faculty, staff, students, and alumni that there is a framework that can help them understand it. Presence, flow, and oscillation are concepts that could be used to frame the holistic experiences students will encounter both inside and outside of the classroom. Ideally, these experiences will be seamless and fluid, allowing students to pursue learning when it is appropriate and when their motivation is highest. It is important that the framework be intentional and visible to students, allowing them to know when they are participating in one or another of the sponsored or funded programs. At every opportunity, the campus culture and the important place of leadership learning would be affirmed. If such a campus culture is established and courses and experiences made available, the hope is that students will participate in increasing numbers and to greater depth.

Frameworks, Frameworks ...

As I indicated in Chapter Six, there are other important structural frameworks to consider when designing leadership programs that advocate creating opportunities to address multiple purposes, strategies, and populations (Roberts, 1981). This and other frameworks are important to consider when addressing the full array of leadership learning opportunity. However, I propose for your consideration the possibility that tapping into students' lived experience may be one of the best ways to design and articulate what is available to them. A framework that students see as reflecting their experience and that provides a road map for the leadership journey is likely the most effective way to attract students and guide them through a loose, but helpful, succession of experiences. Presence, flow, and oscillation are one-word hooks that may be attractive. Seeing, sensing, presencing, envisioning, enacting, and embodying may make more sense to others. Whatever the framework, the language, or the hooks, each educator needs to find a way of articulating to students what the program is about, what opportunities are available within it, and how they can get involved. Ideally, the framework that is used will portray a purposeful and attractive journey that students will be able to recognize as enhancing their collegiate experience.

8

Challenges and Opportunities in Deepening Leadership

I have used the metaphor of a journey several times in the preceding chapters. This is fitting as a way to think of exploring learning and leadership. It is also fitting as a way of portraying what it is like to seek a deeper understanding of leadership and how to develop this critical capacity in ourselves and others. These concluding pages are reflections on the pathway toward, new realizations about, and ultimate destination of leadership in a changing world.

I will begin by reflecting on the roles we play as students, faculty, and staff. I will then acknowledge the inevitable—that nothing of any magnitude unfolds as we would expect. Given that we have relatively little control, what can we do? In the changing and challenging journey of leadership, what are the strategies that keep us on course in pursuit of our goals?

Our Role in the Journey of Deeper Leadership

Students, faculty, and staff share the responsibility for creating the best possible learning and leadership environments. Much of the research and model building that has occurred during the twentieth century substantiates that educationally powerful environments arise from collaborative efforts. Chapter One charted the emergence of faculty and staff roles as higher education became more complex and appealed to broader populations. The modification of these roles and the changing face of higher education in large measure resulted from students' demands for relevance and greater participation. Thus the three groups—students, faculty, and staff—became inextricably linked as the purposes, organization, and focus of higher education changed.

Students

When in the presence of students who have been involved in substantial leadership learning, or in other cases when students may seek change in the ways their colleges function, I've begun to pose the question of whether they see themselves as collectors or contributors. I explain that collectors seek only to accept the lessons and resources others provide and thus assume a passive and unproductive role in the educational process, whereas contributors seek to be teachers as well as learners and thus contribute their own talents and insights in order to effect change. On both logical and experiential grounds, students immediately recognize that, of course, if they want richer and more fulfilling learning and leadership, they have to be involved in shaping and sustaining this commitment.

Leadership Reconsidered: Engaging Higher Education in Social Change (Astin & Astin, 2000) proposed a set of constraining and empowering beliefs that shaped student, faculty, and student affairs staff involvement in leadership. This report emerged from the Social Change Model of Leadership Development that I explained in Chapter Three. In relation to students, the constraining beliefs portrayed a bleak picture of undergraduate life. Personal beliefs about not having time, not feeling welcome to participate, and lacking the status of formal leadership to legitimize their role were the kinds of mindsets that held students back. Given some students' doubts about their ability to lead, a key dilemma arises: How can students help achieve the change they seek if they are unwilling to get involved?

Some students are very willing to engage more deeply in learning and leadership. In the following reflection, one student with whom I've worked expressed beliefs about more inclusive opportunities for leadership and a willingness to take greater responsibility for his own learning:

> Leadership is service. There is no difference between the two. Leadership has nothing to do with title, awards, accomplishment, position; and everything to do with being willing to help other people. It doesn't matter if you're serving food to the homeless or speaking to the Board of Trustees—if you are seeking to serve your community and improve it through your actions then you are a leader no matter what position you may hold.

This sentiment reflects the shift from constraining to empowering beliefs that is so important as students begin to adopt more substantial roles in their learning. In some ways, this kind of shift is likely the result of growing maturity, but it is also the result of experiences and interactions that communicate to students the value and importance of taking responsibility for their own learning.

The beliefs and behaviors that draw students into fuller participation are those more characteristic of adult role models. Growing recognition that they can handle multiple and complex responsibilities, that they are citizens and have civic obligations, and that they are influential are the core assumptions that communicate the importance of full engagement. Another student colleague who is deeply motivated by influencing global change made comments consistent with these beliefs:

> The process of both external and internal surveying caused me to embark on a lifelong mission of what could be described as servant leadership. I have found that leadership is most effective if both the leaders and constituents are seen and treated as equals. Furthermore, that all actions undertaken are for the mutual benefit of all in the community.

Beliefs have great power as inhibitors or activators of involvement but, ultimately, students will make their own choices. The strategy that is likely to have the most positive impact as an invitation to involvement and leadership is one that helps students gain better information about how systems function and how they can most effectively express their voices. Any effort to involve students has to begin with respect and appreciation for the circumstances they encounter. Although there are many critical conditions that we could advocate related to student involvement, one of the most important is to welcome students from all types of experiences and backgrounds. Previous advocacy for women, students of color, and now gay, lesbian, bisexual, and transgender students must be maintained. In addition, if we are to move deeper in leadership learning, students from diverse socioeconomic circumstances, international backgrounds, and students who demonstrate high intellectual intelligence as well as emotional, interpersonal, aesthetic, physical, and spiritual intelligences will need to be included. Ultimately, educators can draw on the Leadership Identity Development research of Komives et al. (2005) to understand how to help all students along their journeys toward finding the leadership potential within themselves. In John's words, "The most lasting lesson from my college years was the importance of instilling a sense of ownership in those you are leading with." Having been a leader of fraternal organizations as an undergraduate and now involved in this type of work in his career, John realized that "the heroic projections of leadership often showcase a tough leader thrusting his/her vision on the followers. I learned that vision is best created, and best achieved, when it is developed and shared by all of those involved in the leadership process." John's view of leadership as a generative and integrated phenomenon resulted in new insights for him and invited others to join in both leadership learning and practice.

Students can make their own place in leadership learning. Faculty and staff also have the power to create circumstances and conditions that help facilitate students' involvement and validate their place as equals in the journey toward effecting true and enduring change.

Faculty

As I indicated in Chapter One, the role of faculty in the academy has changed over time. They served as teachers, mentors, advisers, disciplinarians, and coaches in many educational settings of the eighteenth and nineteenth centuries. Although this role is different today, the sheer longevity of faculty in the academy results in their fulfilling a pivotal position in most colleges and universities. The shift that we presently see under way in faculty participation is from being the sage on the stage to engaging with other learners in a mutual and catalytic way. When learning shifts to engaging with others, positional and expert power is transformed into the power of orchestration that draws contributions out, connects and relates, and provokes deeper considerations. This pedagogy is more aligned with many of the changes we also observe in leadership.

The teaching and learning pedagogies of the past came with baggage, the heaviest being the elitism and privilege of presumed intellectual expertise. The most debilitating impact of old pedagogies is that they keep others at a distance and thus undermine collaborative and participatory learning. Many of the newest models of engaged learning that I included in Chapter One break down conventional views of who holds knowledge both inside and external to the campus community. Privilege can also relate to the actual content of knowledge—the disciplines, applied and professional programs, or emerging transdisciplinary and interdisciplinary relationships we are beginning to see. The competition of disciplines for preeminence has one of its most deleterious effects on leadership studies because leadership as an area of study is young and is so dependent on multiple perspectives. Another form of privilege is longevity—who came to the learning community first and maintains the most consistent role over time? Acknowledging that students were central from the beginning, faculty were the first to have a role in guiding learning within the academy, but does that mean they should claim ultimate authority? Students are only in the community for a short time, whereas faculty and staff are there continuously. Who has the greatest stake, based on what criteria, and how should these vested interests influence decision making? These ideas are packed with implications and fraught with controversy. However, if these issues cannot be explored in honest dialogue, the learning community will continue to be weighted down with burdensome and contentious questions about itself. Unwillingness to address such questions will perpetuate the unrecognized inertia that may be the undoing of the very thing we prize most—the life of learning and the discovery of knowledge.

It seems that letting go of old and heavy bags would be easy, but the familiarity of carrying them has become a habit that remains difficult to change. Still, we stand to gain substantial benefits by carrying a lighter load. The most obvious is that we are freer and more flexible in what we can do. *Leadership Reconsidered* posed important empowering beliefs about more effective ways to share the load of promoting learning and development. How freeing it would be to know that the responsibility for enhancing learning in the academy is a mutual goal for faculty, students, and staff alike. How empowering it would be for faculty to know that they helped to develop leadership potential in students—potential that can result in more in-depth understanding of disciplinary knowledge and greater progress toward career aspirations for their students. By acting on the privilege that faculty maintain, they could begin the process of change immediately. Faculty are in the most influential position to advocate for change and they potentially have the most to gain by doing so. Broadening, sharing, and inviting others to join together only enhances the impact faculty can have in the academy.

One of the most positive and historic aspects of faculty culture is the importance of and seriousness accorded to peer review. Faculty acquired an appreciation for critique of their intellectual and creative property as a way to both recognize the quality of their colleagues' contributions and to increase its quality. This idea is time-honored and preceded the contemporary notion of 360-degree feedback that has taken hold in various for-profit and not-for-profit settings. Peer review, a process that invites colleagues to review and evaluate a faculty member's work, has been one of the factors that has maintained innovation for decades, if not centuries. One interesting and potentially powerful application of this concept could be undertaken in the evaluation of academic and other administrators. If administrative evaluations were constructed with the same commitment to enhancing effectiveness that faculty have used in their tenure and promotion processes, and if leadership was one of the qualities given attention, our colleges and universities might achieve advances never imagined. In many cases, academic and other administrative evaluations have been implicitly based on the heroic model, resulting in challenges to ego and competence that make consideration of change difficult. By contrast, 360-degree collegial review could be constructed to contribute to personal and professional development, resulting in much more able leadership and role modeling in organizations that contribute to the lives of others.

Student Affairs

Chapters One and Two chronicled the emergence of student affairs staff in the academy. These colleagues have now been present in higher education in the United States for more than a century. Other nations around the world have begun to consider creating such roles as well. The problem is that student affairs staff have taken on a separate and unequal role in many, if not most, places. One of the primary purposes I undertook writing *Deeper Learning in Leadership* was to challenge this separation, isolation, and marginalization. If deeper leadership is to unfold through, and as a result of, higher education, our intellectual and organizational models will have to be examined and radically altered so that all educators see themselves serving as leaders and key contributors to the learning process.

Leadership Reconsidered (Astin & Astin, 2000) proposed that some student affairs staff see themselves as second-class citizens whose ideas are underappreciated. In some cases, parents, students, and faculty unintentionally reinforce this belief as they look to student affairs staff to provide high-quality services but not necessarily play a role in promoting learning goals. Student affairs staff themselves likely contribute to the stereotype by remaining hesitant to engage as intellectual partners, research and publish their work, and assume active roles. In essence, such constraining beliefs may have created and perpetuated a dynamic not terribly dissimilar to Moss-Kanter's description of losing streaks (2004). When losing streaks take hold, negativity creeps into an organization's consciousness and creates dysfunction that is clearly pathological. She said, "Of all the pathologies that accumulate in a losing streak, one of the most damaging to individuals, and eventually to the place they work and live, is passivity and learned helplessness" (p. 256). This description characterizes the atmosphere that can develop among student affairs staff whose work is ignored or marginalized. Even if these colleagues are competent and contribute positively to the campus, they may come to believe that their work does not matter—the hallmark of a losing streak—if an institution neglects to recognize and celebrate their accomplishments.

Student affairs staff have the potential to make great contributions to the academy by acting on the belief that learning and development should be viewed holistically, and by seeing themselves as full partners in shaping communities that include and add to the learning of students from all backgrounds.

Mutual Work

How can students, faculty, student affairs staff, and others draw together to pursue deeper learning in leadership? As I proposed, I do not see many other ways than to begin to take more seriously the difficulty of the work before us in enhancing learning and leadership. To be effective, all stakeholders in the process need to help check the compass, visualize and map out the journey, and amass the necessary resources to begin the work. An example of how this could occur may help make this point.

One campus I have observed up close is the institution my younger daughter chose to attend as an undergraduate: Carnegie Mellon University. As a parent of a prospective student, I heard the messages but never imagined the power of what Carnegie Mellon sought to do by tackling learning and leadership both more broadly and deeply. Carnegie Mellon University is a medium-size, private institution with intense academic programs in science and technology, the arts, business, and humanities. Its enrollment is highly selective, with an extraordinarily diverse student population including international and many U.S. cultural groups. Because of its academic intensity, Carnegie Mellon focused primarily on classroom-based learning for most of the twentieth century. What it discovered was that the disciplinary isolation and the bifurcation of intellectual and social learning that had been part of its campus climate had begun to undermine the very qualities of engaged learning it aspired to achieve. This realization sparked a renaissance period during which the institution refocused on undergraduate learning. It has become a campus that maintains academic intensity, relies heavily on fostering interdisciplinary work, balances in-class and out-of-class learning, and focuses deliberately on the value-added outcomes it achieves for students, faculty, staff, and the broader community. Carnegie Mellon has created a niche that is unique in higher education—selective, engaged, boundary-breaking, and innovative. It is a twenty-first-century university that has accomplished enormous change while creating even greater promise. It could not have achieved so much without tackling many of the constraining beliefs with which many institutions struggle. Further, although substantive change is never easy or complete, Carnegie Mellon incorporated into its identity many of the empowering beliefs that *Leadership Reconsidered* encouraged students, faculty, and student affairs to adopt. By taking the risk to go outside conventional views, the institution and all its constituents benefit and thrive.

One of the characteristics that has distinguished Carnegie Mellon for many years has been its commitment to involving students in undergraduate research. With a campus of approximately five thousand undergraduates, the Meeting of the Minds (2006) spring research symposium involved more than four hundred presentations. Moreover, in an age where shrinking global borders have caused other campuses to require students to take foreign languages as part of their undergraduate curriculum, 47 percent of Carnegie Mellon students voluntarily complete the study of a foreign language. Marshall S. Smith, former undersecretary of the U.S. Department of Education, wrote, "Carnegie Mellon is a jewel among the world's universities. It radiates powerful teaching, interdisciplinary research, public service, and a persistent curiosity about all things" (2006).

When my daughter Darbi was invited to offer comments at a graduating senior reception (personal communication, May 18, 2006), she captured the core of the benefits she and her classmates experienced:

> The little "bubble" we like to call campus has allowed us to come into conflict with issues, seek understanding about them, and act without the fear of screwing up. And if we did take a wrong step, our peers and mentors have been there to help us pick up the pieces, move forward, and learn from our mistakes. The past four years have in a sense been "practice" for what we will experience in our lives after college as engaged citizens. That has been invaluable because we've now built up a proverbial "encyclopedia of failures and successes" which we can now access in future times of crises. The most crucial part of the step we'll take from college to the real world is to bring that encyclopedia with us, to make sense of it while we're here, and to carry it proudly hereafter. Only by using the knowledge we've gained

as leaders at Carnegie Mellon can we justify our efforts and our hard work towards making this campus a better place. And by carrying that knowledge with us we are much more likely to prove that we can make a differ-ence in our lives after college as well.

Carnegie Mellon University is an institution that chose to explore new models while preserving historic strengths. It has begun to infuse leadership throughout the university by asking pointed and poignant questions and by engaging students, faculty, and student affairs staff in deep intellectual discourse. This example is likely only one that could demonstrate the importance of joining together in mutual work to enhance learning and leadership in our colleges and universities.

Who's in Charge?

One of the struggles institutions face in advocating for deeper lead-ership learning relates to who will take responsibility or initiative for making changes. The relationships on all campuses are complex and idiosyncratic. Having served at five campuses during my profes-sional journey and consulted on many more, I have realized that there is no prescriptive model, type and number of faculty or staff, nor organizational placement that will ensure success. Fostering effective and deeper leadership learning is highly subjective and dependent on resources. However, I have observed two patterns that I would caution against because they slow down or counter-act positive movement. One is establishing a leadership studies or program director for the campus. Although a coordinating or orchestrating function is desirable, too often a director or chair can be misunderstood as releasing others from their responsibility and interest in leadership learning. The second caution is that, if deeper leadership is the goal, junior and inexperienced staff cannot be charged with the sole responsibility to make it happen. Entry-level staff have wonderful energy, fresh eyes and cutting-edge training, and an openness to change and innovation that are critical resources in the process of working toward deeper learning in leadership. Their lack of experience, frustration in the face of complex organization dynamics, and their lack of face-value credibility with students, faculty, and staff alike limit their ability to garner support and overcome obstacles necessary to achieve optimal gains. Institutions that are serious about deeper leadership must find ways to launch their efforts with credible resources and then work to develop partnerships and acquire more resources to pursue the ever-broadening potential of leadership learning.

Deeper leadership cannot be achieved unless there is a commitment to studying and understanding leadership, which I will address in the following section.

Understanding and Applying Leadership Models

Chapter Three summarized some of the most widely used leadership theories and models. Chapter Four introduced research about preparation and effectiveness for work as a framework for some of the emerging leadership models that I have found most helpful. These two chapters did not presume to cover all the theories and models that readers will eventually find useful. What I hope the chapters did accomplish was to communicate that there are plenty of interesting leadership ideas and that they have great potential in application.

Understanding leadership has to be one of the primary goals of those who wish to deepen leadership learning, but it is an immense challenge when there is so much work to be accomplished. Staying abreast of new models and ideas may be most effectively accomplished by engaging in leadership learning communities that pursue mutual and constant exploration of the theories as they are presented and published. Equally important, leadership educators need to critically analyze and attempt to adapt these new ideas in practice.

Whereas Chapter Four proposed the integration of several leadership models around preparation for employment, Chapter Five proposed another integration around presence, flow, and oscillation. The ideas of presence, flow, and oscillation have heuristic meaning for me. These words, and the philosophical notions and ideas that emerged from them, have practical significance for individuals and organizations. They are not just words or lofty aspirations. Achieving presence in life is a constant and deepening spiral of awareness. Those who have chosen this journey stand out for their authenticity and trustworthiness. Presence and the focus it makes available to us set the stage for enhanced performance that is captured in the word *flow*—continuous movement toward a goal with unrelenting curiosity and persistence. Punctuating intense work and attention with times of renewal sustains high performance that is life-giving to oneself and the organization one serves. Chapter Seven described a variety of programmatic possibilities that could be organized within the ideas of presence, flow, and oscillation. This model may have stimulated new insights or integration of other ideas readers have found helpful. The primary point was to demonstrate that this is the purpose of leadership research and theory—to stimulate our deeper analysis and application of these ideas. The challenge is in staying abreast of the many ideas that could have relevance to the work of leadership learning. The opportunity is that it guarantees a lifetime of interesting reading and translation.

As educators consider leadership models and the approaches to change that I offered in Chapter Six, they must keep in mind that they are pursuing adaptive change (Heifetz, 1994). Adaptive change is not easy. It requires careful and courageous leadership that takes on the issues as well as the processes and experiences we encounter each and every day. Change requires instilling the confidence to take risks and to work toward creating the realities that we hope are possible (Moss-Kanter, 2004). Most of us recognize that the processes we use to create curricular and cocurricular leadership learning are critical and that our relationships are essential to success; however, the fact is that many well-intended and skilled individuals have attempted to build bridges in our academic communities with little success. By coupling connective and inclusive strategies with the excitement of new initiatives in leadership, we may well be able to build bridges with stronger materials and more broad-based support, which will help pave the way toward sustained institutional collaboration.

Nevertheless, sometimes our most well-conceived and best efforts do not go as we anticipate. When the mystery was more than I could decipher, I have found that political and organization dynamics were often a powerful dimension contributing to the surprises. The only choice I had in these situations was to engage with other colleagues and to trust their commitment and purposes. We will be out of control in many of the planning processes we pursue. To pretend or fool ourselves about the quality of our own ability and rightness is self-defeating. Humility is the concept that comes quickly to mind. Humility that envelopes us in every interaction is likely to be appealing to the many stakeholders who would otherwise delight in challenging our intellectual, legitimate, or other authority.

Persistence and Renewal

Persistence and renewal sustained me for thirty years of work in leadership learning and ultimately added to the length and depth of my commitment. My primary way of understanding persistence is to know the impact of presence in my own life. I persist because I am so deeply committed to the goal of understanding leadership and convincing others of the importance of their understanding it as well. I care so deeply about the goal that I will do practically anything to keep others involved. This takes on the form of modifying and incorporating others' ideas throughout the design and delivery of the leadership learning initiatives. This experience is much like students' journeys. As one former student who was a political science, Spanish, and botany major and now works in youth media, Chad Boettcher (personal communication, May 2, 2006), indicated,

> College was about finding myself, my passion, my life. And the biggest challenge for anyone searching for those three mega concepts—is to understand, accept and love what they find. In this is the quest for leadership. For true leaders of all kinds are those who discover who they are, where they are, when they are—and thrive.

Persistence and the success that goes with it envelop all those who are willing to link their pathways together. The pathways need not be identical. The important point is that all those involved can pursue their paths as they see fit and eventually arrive at the end with a shared sense of accomplishment.

I understand renewal to come from the intensity of purposeful work coupled with the breathers that are so necessary to reenergize me. Flow and oscillation are other words I used to describe this process of renewal. The challenge is adopting these as a way of life, much like a rhythmic pattern that shapes a piece of music gathering tempo and momentum. Our leadership learning rhythm may include diversions of self-criticism and critical analyses resulting from assessment and continuous improvement. Movement back and forth between acting and reflecting, implementing and assessing, and advancing and regrouping are characteristic of healthy learning organizations and communities.

Ultimately, renewing and sustaining deeper leadership might be captured by observing the three principles Richard Boyatzis and Annie McKee (2006) propose: mindfulness, hope, and compassion. These three wonderfully simple words convey a constant yearning for understanding that is informed by critical thinking, a commitment to optimism and possibility, and a connection to our fellow travelers along life's pathway. With these principles to frame the process, and deeper leadership as the goal, we can transform ourselves and thereby our institutions. We can become the catalysts and our institutions can become the environments in which learning and leadership thrive.

References

American Association of Higher Education, American College Personnel Association, & National Association of Student Personnel Administrators. (1998). *Powerful partnerships: A shared responsibility for learning.* Washington, DC: Author.

American College Personnel Association. (1994). *The student learning imperative: Implications for student affairs.* Washington, DC: Author.

American Council on Education. (1937). The student personnel point of view. Reprinted in G. Saddlemire & A. Rents (Eds.) (1984), *Student affairs—a profession's heritage: Significant articles, authors, issues and documents* (pp. 74–87). Carbondale, IL: American College Personnel Association.

American Council on Education. (1949). The student personnel point of view (Rev. ed.). Reprinted in G. Saddlemire & A. Rents (Eds.) (1984), *Student affairs—a profession's heritage: Significant articles, authors, issues and documents* (pp. 122–140). Carbondale, IL: American College Personnel Association.

American Psychological Association. (2007). Leadership [Special issue]. *American Psychologist, 62*(1).

Arendt, H. (1949). *The origins of totalitarianism.* Orlando: Harcourt.

Association of American Colleges and Universities. (2002). *Greater expectations: A new vision for learning as a nation goes to college.* Washington, DC: Author.

Astin, A. W. (1993). *What matters in college: Four critical years revisited.* San Francisco: Jossey-Bass.

Astin, A. W. (1999). "Involvement in learning" revisited: Lessons we have learned. *Journal of College Student Development, 49,* 587–598.

Astin, A. W., & Astin, H. S. (Eds.). (2000). *Leadership reconsidered: Engaging higher education in social change.* Battle Creek, MI: W. K. Kellogg Foundation.

Astin, H. S., & Leland, C. (1991). *Women of influence, women of vision: A cross-generational study of leaders and social change.* San Francisco: Jossey-Bass.

Banta, T. W. (2006). Reliving the history of large-scale assessment in higher education. *Assessment Update, 18*(4), 3–4, 15.

Banta, T. W., & Pike, G. R. (2007). Revisiting the blind alley of value added. *Assessment Update, 19*(1), 1–2, 14–15.

Bass, B. M. (1985). *Leadership and performance beyond expectations.* New York: Free Press.

Bass, B. M., & Avolio, B. J. (Eds.). (1994). *Improving organizational effectiveness through transformational leadership.* Thousand Oaks, CA: Sage.

Bass, B. M., & Avolio, B. J. (1995). *Multifactor leadership questionnaire* (2nd ed.). Redwood City, CA: Mindgarden.

Baxter Magolda, M. B. (2004). Learning Partnerships Model: A framework for promoting self-authorship. In M. B. Baxter Magolda & P. M. King (Eds.), *Learning partnerships: Theory and models of practice to educate for self-authorship* (pp. 37–62). Sterling, VA: Stylus.

Bensimon, E. M., Neumann, A., & Birnbaum, R. (1989). *Making sense of administrative leadership: The "L" word in higher education. ASHE-ERIC Higher Education Report.* San Francisco: Jossey-Bass.

Berkowitz, A. D. (1998). The proactive prevention model: Helping students translate healthy beliefs into healthy actions. *About Campus, 3*(4), 26–27.

Brungardt, C., & Crawford, C. B. (1996). A comprehensive approach to assessing leadership students and programs: Preliminary findings. *Journal of Leadership Studies, 3*, 37–48.

Bulger, P. G. (1954). Financial realities and resources. In E. Lloyd-Jones & M. R. Smith (Eds.), *Student personnel work as deeper teaching* (pp. 215–226). New York: HarperCollins.

Burns, J. M. (1978). *Leadership*. New York: HarperCollins.

Burns, J. M. (2003). *Academy of Leadership*. Retrieved April 19, 2006, from www.academy.umd.edu/aboutus/staff/JBurns.htm.

Business Development Directives and Garrett Consulting. (2005). *Employer survey of graduates effectiveness*. Unpublished manuscript, Office of Career Services, Miami University, Oxford, Ohio.

Council for the Advancement of Standards (CAS). (1996). *Student leadership program standards*. Retrieved May 19, 2006, from www.cas.edu.

Covey, S. (2004). *The 8th habit*. New York: Free Press.

Csikszentmihalyi, M. (1993). *The evolving self: A psychology for the third millennium*. New York: HarperCollins.

Csikszentmihalyi, M. (2003). *Good business: Leadership, flow, and the making of meaning*. New York: Penguin.

Dewey, J. (1923). *Democracy and education*. New York: Macmillan.

Downton, J. V., Jr. (1973). *Rebel leadership: Commitment and charisma in the revolutionary process*. New York: Free Press.

Ehrlich, T. (1997). Dewey versus Hutchins: The next round. In R. Orrill (Ed.), *Education and democracy: Re-imagining liberal learning in America* (pp. 225–262). New York: College Entrance Examination Board.

Ehrlich, T. (1999). Civic and moral learning. *About Campus, 4*(4), 5–9.

Evans, N. J., & Reason, R. D. (2001). Philosophical statements. *Journal of College Student Development, 42,* 359–377.

Evers, F., Power, B., & Mitchell, J. (2003, May). *Preparing for the future: Identifying advanced essential skills needs in Canada. A report of the Advanced Level Essential Skills Project Steering Committee.* Ottawa: Canadian Alliance of Education and Training Organizations.

Evers, F. T., Rush, J. C., & Berdrow, I. (1998). *The bases of competence: Skills for lifelong learning and employability.* San Francisco: Jossey-Bass.

Fowler, J. W. (1981). *Stages of faith: The psychology of human development and the quest for meaning.* San Francisco: Harper San Francisco.

The Gallup Organization. (2005). *Strengths finder.* Retrieved December 3, 2005, from www.strengthsfinder.com.

Gardner, J. (1990). *On leadership.* New York: Free Press.

Gilligan, C. (1982). *In a different voice: Psychological theory and women's development.* Cambridge, MA: Harvard University Press.

Gladwell, M. (2005). *Blink: The power of thinking without thinking.* New York: Time Warner.

Glover, S., & Wilson, M. (2006). *Unconventional wisdom: A brief history of CCL's pioneering research and innovation.* Greensboro, NC: Center for Creative Leadership.

Goethals, G., & Sorenson, G. (General Eds.), & Burns, J. M. (Senior Ed.). (2004). *Encyclopedia of leadership* (4 vols.). Thousand Oaks, CA: Sage.

Goethals, G., & Sorenson, G. (Eds.). (2006). *The quest for a general theory of leadership.* Northampton, MA: Edward Elgar.

Goleman, D., Boyatzis, R., & McKee, A. (2002). *Primal leadership: Learning to lead with emotional intelligence.* Boston: Harvard Business School Press.

Greenleaf, R. K. (1977). *Servant leadership: A journey into the nature of legitimate power and greatness.* New York: Paulist Press.

Greenleaf, R. K., & Spears, L. C. (2002). *Servant leadership: A journey into the nature of legitimate power and greatness* (25th anniversary ed.). New York: Paulist Press.

Hagberg, J. O. (2003). *Real power: Stages of personal power in organizations* (3rd ed.). Salem, WI: Sheffield.

Hannum, M. K., Martineau, J. W., & Reinelt, C. (Eds.). (2006). *The handbook of leadership development evaluation*. San Francisco: Jossey-Bass.

Harter, N. H. (2005, November 20). *62 books on leadership*. Message posted to International Leadership Association ILA-Exchange, archived at https://listserv. umd.edu/archives/ila-exchange.html.

Heifetz, R. A. (1994). *Leadership without easy answers*. Cambridge, MA: Belknap Press.

Heifetz. R. A., & Laurie, D. L. (2001). The work of leadership. In G. Goleman, W. Peace, W. Pagonis, T. Peters, G. Jones, & H. Collingwood (Eds.), *Harvard Business Review on breakthrough leadership* (pp. 131–141). Boston: Harvard Business School Press.

Heifetz, R. A., & Linsky, M. (2002). *Leadership on the line: Staying alive through the dangers of leading*. Boston: Harvard Business School Press.

Helgesen, S. (1990). *Women's ways of leading*. New York: Doubleday.

Helgesen, S. (1995). *The female advantage: Women's ways of leadership*. New York: Doubleday.

Higher Education Research Institute. (1994). *A social change model of leadership development, guidebook version II*. Los Angeles: Higher Education Research Institute.

Higher Education Research Institute. (1996). *Guidebook for a social change model of leadership development*. Los Angeles: Graduate School of Education and Information Studies, University of California.

Howe, W. (2005, November 20). *Growing discipline of organization leadership*. Message posted to International Leadership Association ILA-Exchange, archived at https://listserv.umd.edu/archives/ila-exchange.html.

Inscape Publishing. (2001). DiSC Classic (Version 9.0). Minneapolis, MN: Author.

Keeling, R. P. (1998). HIV/AIDS in the academy: Engagement and learning in a context of change. *NASPA Leadership for a Healthy Campus, 1,* 1–8.

Kegan, R. (1994). *In over our heads: The mental demands of modern life.* Cambridge, MA: Harvard University Press.

Kellerman, B. (2001). Required reading. *Harvard Business Review, 79*(11), 15–24.

Kellerman, B. (2004). *Bad leadership: What it is, how it happens, why it matters (Leadership for the common good).* Cambridge, MA: Harvard University Press.

Kezar, A., Carducci, R., & Contreras-McGavin, M. (2006). *Rethinking the "L" word in higher education: The revolution of research on leadership: ASHE Higher Education Report.* San Francisco: Jossey-Bass.

King, M. L., Jr. (1964). "Letter from Birmingham Jail." Retrieved February 24, 2006, from www.nobelprizes.com/nobel/peace/MLK-jail.html.

Komives, S. R., & Dugan, J. (2006). *Multi-Institution Study of Leadership.* College Park, MD: National Clearinghouse for Leadership Programs.

Komives, S. R., Dugan, J., Owen, J. E., & Slack, C. (Eds.). (2006). *Handbook for student leadership programs.* College Park, MD: National Clearinghouse for Leadership Programs.

Komives, S. R., Lucas, N., & McMahon, T. R. (1998). *Exploring leadership: For college students who want to make a difference.* San Francisco: Jossey-Bass.

Komives, S. R., Lucas, N., & McMahon, T. R. (2007). *Exploring leadership: For college students who want to make a difference* (2nd ed.). San Francisco: Jossey-Bass.

Komives, S. R., Owen, J. E., Longerbeam, S., Mainella, F. C., & Osteen, L. (2005). Developing a leadership identity: A grounded theory. *Journal of College Student Development, 46,* 593–611.

Kouzes, J. M., & Posner, B. Z. (1987). *The leadership challenge: How to get extraordinary things done in organizations.* San Francisco: Jossey-Bass.

Kouzes, J. M., & Posner, B. Z. (1988). *The Leadership Practices Inventory*. San Diego: Pfeiffer.

Kouzes, J. M., & Posner, B. Z. (2002). *The leadership challenge* (3rd ed.). San Francisco: Jossey-Bass.

Kouzes, J. M., & Posner, B. Z. (2005). *Student Leadership Practices Inventory—self*. San Francisco: Jossey-Bass.

Kouzes, J. M., & Posner, B. Z. (2006). *Student leadership planner: An action guide to achieving your personal best*. San Francisco: Jossey-Bass.

Kuh, G. D., Kinzie, J., Schuh, J. H., Whitt, E. J., & Associates. (2005). *Student success in college: Creating conditions that matter*. San Francisco: Jossey-Bass.

Kuhn, T. S. (1970). *The structure of scientific revolutions* (2nd ed.). Chicago: University of Chicago Press.

LeMay, N. V., & Ellis, A. (2006). Evaluating leadership development and organizational performance. In M. K. Hannum, J. W. Martineau, & C. Reinelt (Eds.), *The handbook of leadership development evaluation*. San Francisco: Jossey-Bass.

Lindsay, R., Robins, K., & Terrel, R. (2003). *Cultural proficiency: A manual for school leaders* (2nd ed.). Thousand Oaks, CA: Corwin.

Lipman-Blumen, J. (1996). *The connective edge*. San Francisco: Jossey-Bass.

Lipman-Blumen, J. (2004). *The allure of toxic leaders: Why we follow destructive bosses and corrupt politicians—and how we can survive them*. Oxford: Oxford University Press.

Lloyd-Jones, E., & Smith, M. R. (1954). *Student personnel work as deeper teaching*. New York: HarperCollins.

Machiavelli, N. (1954). *The Prince* (N. H. Thompson, Trans.). New York: Limited Editions Club. (Original work published 1513)

Magolda, P. M. (2005). Proceed with caution: Uncommon wisdom about academic and student affairs partnerships. *About Campus*, 9(6), 16–21.

Matusak, L. (2005). Principles of collaborative leadership. In *News & tools: Leadership*. College Park, MD: James MacGregor Burns Academy of Leadership, University of Maryland.

McKee, A., & Boyatzis, R. E. (2006). Renewing and sustaining leadership. *Leader to Leader, 40*, 30–36.

Meeting of the minds. (2006). Retrieved May 24, 2006, from www.cmu.edu/cmnews/extra/040504_meetingofminds.html.

Meyers, R. (2006). Lessons from building service-learning. In E. Zlotkowski, N. V. Longo, & J. R. Williams (Eds.), *Students as colleagues: Expanding the circle of service-learning leadership*. Providence, RI: Campus Compact.

Moss-Kanter, R. B. (2004). *Confidence: How winning streaks and losing streaks begin and end*. New York: Crown Business.

Myers & Briggs Foundation. (2006). *Myers-Briggs type indicator*. Retrieved May 11, 2006, from www.myersbriggs.org.

Nadler, L. (1970). *Developing human resources*. Houston: Gulf.

Nash, R. J. (2002). *"Real world" ethics: Frameworks for educators and human service professionals* (2nd ed.). New York: Teachers College Press.

National Association of Student Personnel Administrators & American College Personnel Association. (2004). *Learning reconsidered: A campus-wide focus on the student experience*. Retrieved on November 1, 2005, from www.myacpa.org/pub/pub_othermedia.cfm.

Northouse, P. (2004). *Leadership: Theory and practice* (3rd ed.). Thousand Oaks, CA: Sage.

Nuss, E. M. (2003). The development of student affairs. In S. R. Komives & D. B Woodard Jr. (Eds.), *Student services: A handbook for the profession* (4th ed.). San Francisco: Jossey-Bass.

Osteen, L. (2005, November). *Best practices in leadership development: What has LeaderShape learned in 20 years?* Presentation to the International Leadership Association conference, Amsterdam.

O'Toole, J. (2005). Warren Bennis and the rise of leadership studies. *Compass*. Cambridge, MA: Center for Public Leadership: John F. Kennedy School of Government, Harvard University.

Outcalt, C. L., Faris, S. K., & McMahon, K. N. (2001). *Developing non-hierarchical leadership on campus: Case studies and best practices in higher education*. Westport, CT: Greenwood Press.

Palmer, P. J. (1990). *The active life*. San Francisco: Harper.

Parks, S. D. (2000). *Big questions, worthy dreams*. San Francisco: Jossey-Bass.

Parks, S. D. (2005). *Leadership can be taught*. San Francisco: Jossey-Bass.

Perry, W., Jr. (1970). *Intellectual and ethical development in the college years*. New York: Holt, Rinehart, & Winston.

Perry, W. G. (1998). *Forms of ethical and intellectual development in the college years: A scheme*. San Francisco: Jossey-Bass.

Phillips, J. J., & Phillips, P. (2006). Measuring return on investment in leadership development. In M. K. Hannum, J. W. Martineau, & C. Reinelt (Eds.), *The handbook of leadership development evaluation*. San Francisco: Jossey-Bass.

Putman, R. (2000). *Bowling alone*. New York: Simon & Schuster.

Quinley, H. (2005). *National leadership index 2005: A national study of confidence in leadership*. Report prepared by the Segmentation Company, a division of Yankelovich, for *U.S. News & World Report* & Center for Public Leadership, John F. Kennedy School of Government, Harvard University.

Roberts, D. C. (Ed.). (1981). *Student leadership programs in higher education*. Washington, DC: American College Personnel Association.

Roberts, D. C. (Producer). (1988). Esther Lloyd-Jones on student personnel values [videotape]. Poughkeepsie, NY: American College Personnel Association.

Roberts, D. C. (1998). Student learning was always supposed to be the core of our work—what happened? *About Campus*, 3(3), 18–22.

Roberts, D. C. (2003). Crossing the boundaries in leadership program design. In C. Cherrey, J. J. Gardiner, & N. Huber (Eds.), *Building leadership bridges* (pp. 137–149). College Park, MD: International Leadership Association.

Roberts, D. C., & Huffman, E. (2005). Learning citizenship: Campus-based initiatives for developing student change agents. *About Campus, 10*(4), 17–22.

Roberts, D. C., & Rogers, J. L. (2003). Transforming fraternal leadership. In D. Gregory (Ed.), *The administration of fraternal organizations on North American campuses: A pattern for the new millennium.* Asheville, NC: College Administration Publications.

Roberts, D. C., & Ullom, C. (1989). Student Leadership Program Model. *NASPA Journal, 1,* 67–74.

Rost, J. (1991). *Leadership for the twenty-first century.* New York: Praeger.

Rost, J. (1993). Leadership development in the new millennium. *Journal of Leadership Studies, 1*(1), 91–110.

Rudolph, F. (1962). *The American college and university: A history.* New York: Knopf.

Schroeder, D. A., Penner, L. A., Dovidio, J. F., & Piliavin, J. A. (1995). *The psychology of helping and altruism: Problems and puzzles.* New York: McGraw-Hill.

Schwartz, T., & Loehr, J. (2001). The making of a corporate athlete. *Harvard Business Review, 79*(1), 120–128.

Senge, P., Scharmer, C. O., Jaworski, J., & Flowers, B. S. (2004). *Presence: Human purpose and the field of the future.* Cambridge, MA: Society for Organizational Learning.

Smith, M. S. (2006). *The innovative university.* Retrieved May 24, 2006, from www.cmu.edu/innovativeuniversity.

Spanier, G. (2006, April 28). *A more holistic college experience: Inauguration of Pasquerilla Spiritual Center.* Retrieved December 21, 2006, from http://president. psu.edu/speeches/articles/pasquerilla.html.

Sternberg, R. J. (2007). A systems model of leadership. *American Psychologist*, *62*, 34–42.

Stoecker, R. (2004, May). *Creative tensions in the new community based research*. Prepared for the Community-Based Research Network Symposium, Carleton University, Ottawa, Canada.

Taylor, K. B. (2005). A gathering of great minds: Designing twenty-first century education with twentieth century ideas. *About Campus, 10*(2), 17–23.

Thelin, J. R. (2003). Historical overview of American higher education. In S. R. Komives & D. B. Woodard Jr. (Eds.), *Student services: A handbook for the profession* (4th ed.). San Francisco: Jossey-Bass.

Tutu, D. *Ubuntu*. (1999). Retrieved December 1, 2005, from http://en.wikipedia.org/wiki/Ubuntu_(ideology).

Tyree, T. M. (1998). *Designing an instrument to measure socially responsible leadership using the Social Change Model of Leadership Development*. Unpublished doctoral dissertation, University of Maryland, College Park.

Villa-Vicencio, C. (1996). *Spirit of freedom: South African leaders on religion and politics*. Berkeley: University of California Press.

Wilber, K. (2000). *A theory of everything: An integral vision for business, politics, science and spirituality*. Boston: Shambhala.

Wilber, K., & Scharmer, O. (2003). *Mapping the integral U*. Retrieved May 11, 2006, from www.dialogonleadership.org/wilber.htm.

Wren, T. (1995). *The leader's companion*. New York: Free Press.

Zimmerman-Oster, K., & Burkhardt, J. C. (1999). *Leadership in the making: Impact and insights from leadership development programs in U.S. colleges and universities*. Battle Creek, MI: W. K. Kellogg Foundation.

Index